HANDBOOK ON C LANGUAGE

HANDBOOK ON C LANGUAGE

By

Sangita Sardana

Lecturer, Deptt. of Computer Science

DAV School, Chandigarh

FIREWALL MEDIA

(An Imprint of Laxmi Publications Pvt. Ltd.)

BANGALORE • CHENNAI • COCHIN • GUWAHATI • HYDERABAD
JALANDHAR • KOLKATA • LUCKNOW • MUMBAI • RANCHI
NEW DELHI • BOSTON, USA

Published by :
FIREWALL MEDIA
(An Imprint of Laxmi Publications Pvt. Ltd.)
113, Golden House, Daryaganj,
New Delhi-110002

Phone : 011-43 53 25 00
Fax : 011-43 53 25 28

www.laxmipublications.com
info@laxmipublications.com

First Edition : 2013

OFFICES

✆ **Bangalore**	080-26 75 69 30	✆ **Chennai**	044-24 34 47 26
✆ **Cochin**	0484-237 70 04, 405 13 03	✆ **Guwahati**	0361-254 36 69, 251 38 81
✆ **Hyderabad**	040-24 65 23 33	✆ **Jalandhar**	0181-222 12 72
✆ **Kolkata**	033-22 27 43 84	✆ **Lucknow**	0522-220 95 78
✆ **Mumbai**	022-24 91 54 15, 24 92 78 69	✆ **Ranchi**	0651-221 47 64

FCL–3079–195–HANDBOOK ON C LANGUAGE–SAR C—

Typeset at : ABRO Enterprises, Delhi. Printed at : Repro Knowledgecast Limited, Thane

Contents

PREFACE

I am highly glad to present a series on computer languages. Writing a book to serve students community, gives a great feeling of satisfaction. Various books on high level languages are available in the market but it has been my desire to present such a series on computer languages which could serve the students community in some different manner which could be well acceptable by all. Generally students feel that the books available on the high do not cater to their requirements and there is a dearth of programming examples and graded programs. With the inspiration provided by my students. I have been able to frame a series of four different computer languages C, C++, Java and Visual Basic. Presentation in all the four books is almost on the similar lines.

This treatise covers chapters in uniform manner *i.e.,* from beginning level to advanced level of **C language.** Advanced topics like Files, Linked Lists, Stacks, Queues etc., have been explained in an understandable manner. Each and every topic has been explained with examples and illustrations.

A sufficient number of programming examples has been provided in the book after the topics and as a separate portion in the form of "More Worked-Out Examples". Actual screen shots have been given both with program listings and output run.

All efforts have been made to provide the text in an error-free form yet there is a chance within human limitations that some error might have crept in inadvertently. Readers are requested to brought such errors in our notice so that future edition of this book could be improved.

—Author

Chapter 1 Introduction to C

C is a popular high level programming language with a large library of various types of functions. It is a very popular language among programmers due to its multiple features.

CHARACTERISTICS OF C

1. C is ideally suited for development of reusable software. This helps in cost reduction of software development.
2. C is highly flexible language with versatility. It can be used for developing system software viz., operating systems compilers, editors and data bases. The dBASE program has been written in C language.
3. Since C is a machine independent language, there is no need of re-written software at the time when a computer is upgraded.

CHARACTERS USED IN C

The set of characters used in C consists of alphabet, digits and special characters.

The following table represents the characters used in this language :

Letters :	A B C D E F G............X Y Z
	a b c d e f g...................x y z
Numeric Digits :	0 1 2 3 4 5 6 7 8 9
Special Characters :	
(*i*) Arithmetic Operators	–, +, *, /, %
(*ii*) Logical Operators	&, !
(*iii*) Brackets	() {} [ ]
(*iv*) Relational Operators	<> = #
(*v*) Other Symbols	: ; _ (underscore) >> ?

C TOKENS

The group of characters that logically belong together is called token. Tokens are of four types :

1. Identifiers
2. Keywords
3. Constants
4. Operators

Identifiers

A program can use various data items with symbolic names in C. Identifiers refer to the names of functions, arrays, variables, classes etc., created by a programmer. There are certain rules for naming these identifiers. An identifier, generally contains symbolic name. These symbolic names are used in various C programs.

Rules for Naming Identifiers

1. Uppercase letters and lower case letters are distinct. For example LAXMI and laxmi are different.
2. The name of identifier cannot begin with a digit. 1LAXMI is an invalid name. However, the first character can be selected as an underscore (_).
3. Only alphabetic characters, digits and underscore (_) are permitted in this language.
4. No other special character is allowed for naming a variable.
5. A keyword cannot be used as a variable name.

It is essential to declare variables before their usage in the program. A declaration statement lists the type and number of the variable.

For example

`int i = 0;`	Here `i` is declared as integer and has been initialized with a value of 0.
`char name`	Here name is character variable.
`float sale`	Here sale is a floating point variable.

Keywords

In C keywords are reserved identifiers which cannot be used as names for the variables in a program. The set of C keywords has been given in the following list :

asm	double	new	swithch
auto	else	operator	template
break	enum	private	this
case	extern	protected	throw
catch	float	public	try
char	for	register	typedef
class	friend	return	union
const	goto	short	unsigned
continue	if	signed	virtual
default	inline	sizeof	void
delete	int	static	volatile
delete	long	struct	while

Constants

As evident from the name, an item whose value is not changed during the execution of the program is called constant. If you try to change the value, the program will not successfully execute and generate errors. Each constant is determined by its value and form. C has three types of constants.

(*i*) Numeric Constant

(*ii*) Character Constant

(*iii*) String Constant

Operators

An operator is a symbol or letter which causes the compiler to take an action and yield a value. An operator acts on different data items/entities called **Operands.**

For example, a + b is an expression in which sign + is an operator which specifies the operation of addition.

A detailed discussion on operators has been given in a separate chapter.

The logical expression returns 1 if the result is true and it returns 0 if the result is false.

C provides three logical operators which are listed below :

Symbol	*Meaning*
!	Logical negation (Logical inverse)
||	Logical OR
&&	Logical AND

COMMENTS

Comments are explanation of program (what the program will do) or any other function within a program. A program may be simple to the programmer who has written it, but may be complex for others if he does not include comments in the programs. Comments increase the readability and understandability of the programs. Comments can be used anywhere in the programs but comments lines are not executed in the program.

Comments can be written in the following styles :

```
// or between the pair/*.............*/
/* is the beginning of the comment and
/* is the end of the comment.
```

Look at the following program :

Program

```
//This program adds two numbers
#include<stdio.h>
main()
```

```
    {
        int a,b,c;
        c = a + b;
        printf("",c);
}
        }     //end of the program        (Comments line)
```

The first line in the above program *i.e.,* // This program adds two numbers is a comment. Similarly, the last line *i.e.,*// end of the program is also a comment.

You can also use multi-line comments in the programs. When a comment exceeds one line, you can write it between /* and */.

A FIRST PROGRAM

Type the following program into your favourite editor :

Program

```
#include<stdio.h>
void main()
{
    printf("\nHello World\n");
}
```

Save the code in the file `hello.c`, then compile it.

This creates an *executable* file, which is then executed simply by typing its name. The result is that the characters `"Hello World"` are printed out, preceded by an empty line.

A C program contains *functions* and *variables.* The functions specify the tasks to be performed by the program. The `"main"` function establishes the overall logic of the code. It is normally kept short and calls different functions to perform the necessary sub-tasks. All C codes must have a `"main"` function.

Our `hello.c` code calls `printf`, an output function from the I/O (input/output) library (defined in the file `stdio.h`). The original C language did not have any built-in I/O statements whatsoever. Nor did it have much arithmetic functionality. These functions are now performed by standard libraries, which are now part of ANSI C. The K & R textbook lists the content of these and other standard libraries in an appendix.

The `printf` line prints the message `"Hello World"` on `"stdout"` (the output stream corresponding to the X-terminal window in which you run the code); `"\n"` prints a "new line" character, which brings the cursor onto the next line. By construction, `printf` never inserts this character on its own : the following program would produce the same result :

Program

```
#include <stdio.h>

void main()
{
    printf("\n");
```

```
    printf("Hello world");
    printf("\n");
}
```

The first statement "#include <stdio.h>" includes a specification of the C I/O library. All variables in C must be explicitly defined before use : ".h" files are by convention "header files" which contain definitions of variables and functions necessary for the functioning of a program, whether it be in a user-written section of code, or as part of the standard C libraries. The directive "#include" tells the C compiler to insert the contents of the specified file at that point in the code. The "<. . .>" notation instructs the compiler to look for the file in certain "standard" system directories.

The void preceeding "main" indicates that main is of "void" type -- that is, it has no type associated with it, meaning that it cannot return a result on execution.

The ";"denotes the end of a statement. Blocks of statements are put in braces {...}, as in the definition of functions. All C statements are defined in free format without any specified layout. The following program would produce exactly the same result as our earlier example :

```
#include<stdio.h>
void main() {printf("\nHello World\n");}
```

The reason for arranging your programs in lines and indenting is to increase readability.

ERROR MESSAGE

While writing C programs, various types of errors can happen. These errors are of 3 types :

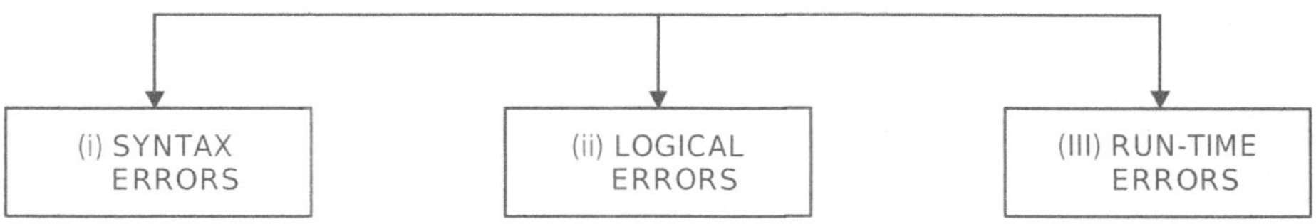

Fig. 1.1

Syntax Errors

Syntax Errors occur due to violation of syntax rules in C. Programs having syntax errors do not execute. It is necessary to remove these errors. C compiler locates these errors and these can be removed.

Logical Errors

Logical errors occur due to wrong use of logic, *i.e.,* formulae. Programs having logical errors can execute and compile, but the result obtained is not correct. To locate these errors the programmers has to study the program carefully. These errors cannot be located by compilers.

Run-Time Errors

Run-time Errors occur when the operation can't be performed during execution. Programs having run-time errors can compile but can't produce meaningful results.

Illustration : *The following program has errors. Locate the errors.*

Program

```
//This program finds the square of an integer
#include<stdio.h>
main()
{
    int number:
    puts("Enter the number")
    scanf("%d", &number);
    square = (number * number)
    printf ("Square of the number=%d\n", square);
    return 0;
}
```

Solution

```
//This program finds square of the number.
#include<stdio.h>
main( )
{
int number;
puts("Enter the number:")
scanf("%d", &number);
square = (number *number);
printf("Square of the number=%d\n", square);
return 0;
}
```

This program does not compile successfully. The compiler shows the following error messages.

Error : `Expression syntax in function main( )`

Error : `Undefined syntax "square in main function( )`

1. The actual error is in the following statement:

   `puts ("Enter the number :")`

   In this statement, the semi-colon is missing.
2. The second message points error in the following statements:

   `square = (number * number);`

The error message states that the identifier has not been declared in the program. You will have to define it as `int number, square`.

USE OF EDITOR

The editor allows the user to type and edit the program. The program which has been created by the help of an editor is called a **Source Program** or **Source Code.**

A C program can be created on DOS by any editor such as WordStar, Word Processor, NE etc. The WordStar cursor commands can be used for the purpose of editing.

If you have turbo C program in TC directory, then the following steps can be used :

1. The screen of the computer shows the following :

    C : \ > CD TC ↵

    C : \ TC> CD BIN ↵

2. Invoke Turbo C by entering TC.

    C : \TC\BIN> TC ↵

After executing the above command, you can load a file in the memory. You have to give it. CPP extension.

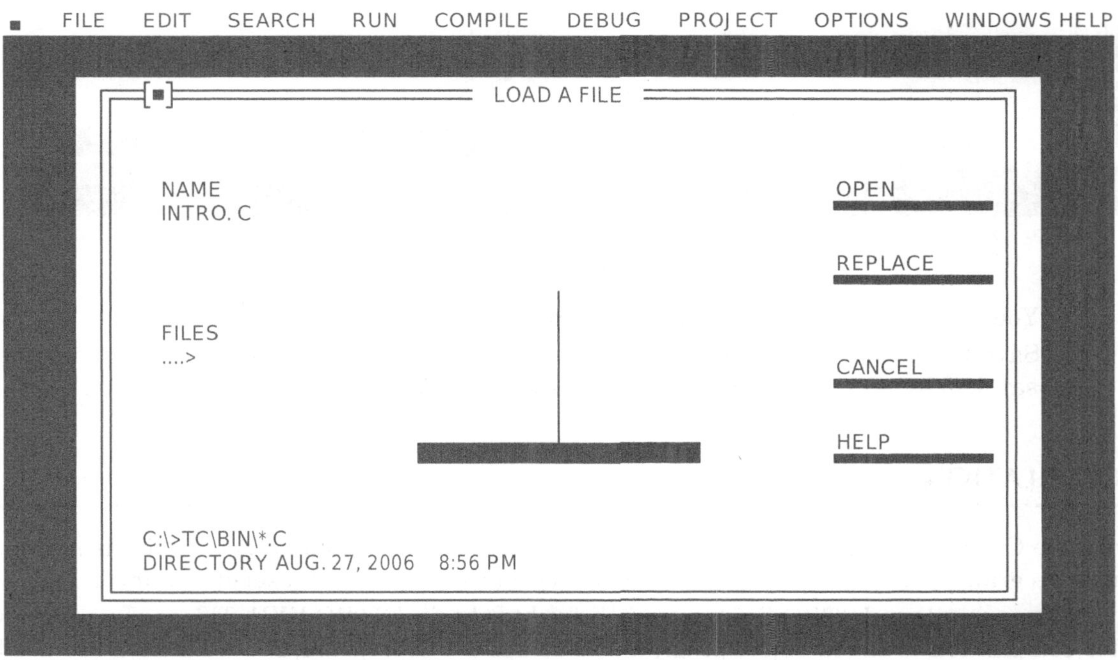

Fig. 1.2

After typing the name you will reach at the Text window.

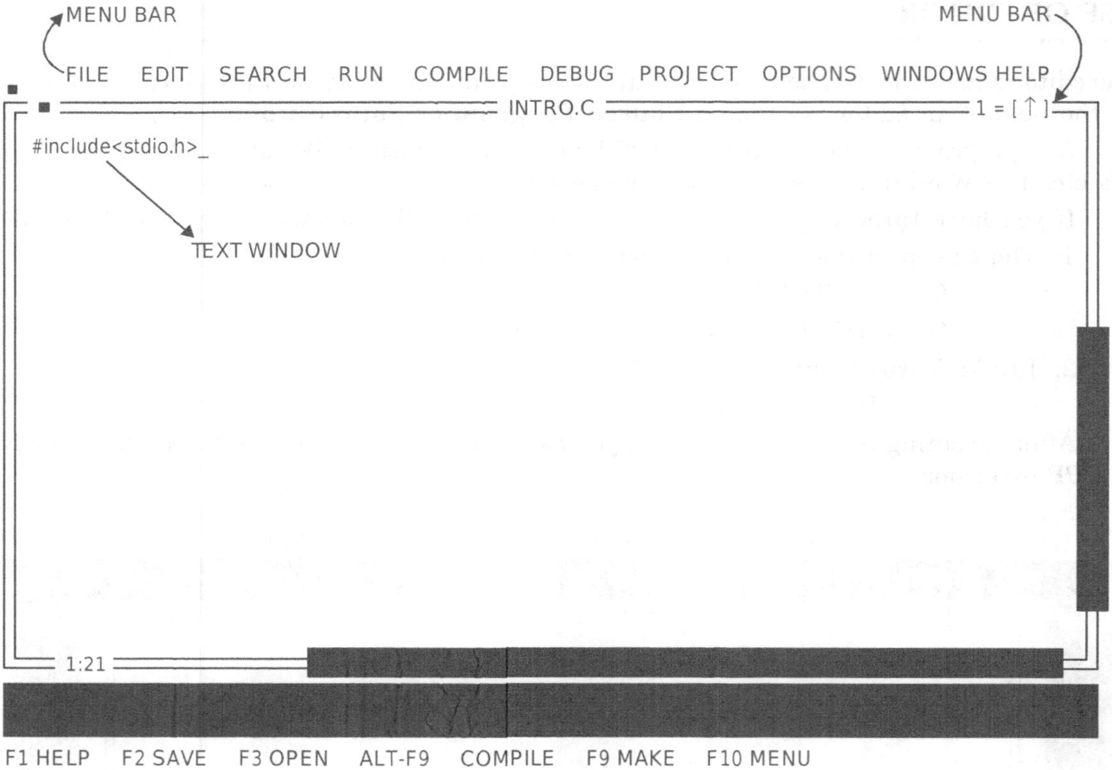

Fig. 1.3

3. You can type (write) the program in text window.
4. Save the program by pressing [F2] key. For saving, you can choose a suitable name, say INTRO.C. The extension indicates that "INTRO" is a C program.

COMPILATION

Once the C program is created, it is compiled with the help of compiler. A compiler is nothing but a program which translates the source program into machine executable form.

After compiling, INTRO.C program is linked to obtain INTRO.EXE. The source program after compilation is called object program. To compile a C program, Alt + F9 keys are used.

Linking

Mostly the programs use built-in function. These functions are also called **library** functions. The linker is used to link these functions with the object program. After linking the object Program is called Final Executable Program or Module. To make a executable file, F9 key is pressed.

Execution

The final executable program can be executed to obtain the output.

Escape Sequence

C has some special character constants, which are called backslash character constants. The escape sequence contains a backslash (\) followed by a character. The following are the important backslash character constants.

\b	back-space
\t	tab
\a	bell (sound)
\n	newline character
\r	carriage return
\u	tale (vertical)
\o	NULL
\f	form feed

A brief detail of these backslash characters is given below.

\b backspace

This character is called backspace character. It is equivalent to pressing backspace key on the key board.

Illustration :

```
#include<stdio.h>
main()
{
   printf("POONAM\b");
}
```

Output of the above program will be POONA.

\t tab

This character is called tab character. When \t is inserted in output statement, the display of the output takes place at the different tab stops.

Illustration :

```
#include<stdio.h>
main()
{
   printf("NEW\t");
   printf("PUBLICATIONS\t");
   printf("NEW DELHI");
}
```

Output of the above program

NEW PUBLICATIONS NEW DELHI

\n tab

This character is used for new line. When \n is inserted in output statement, the next output takes a new line.

\a alert

This character is called bell (alert) character. When \a is used with the output statement, it produces a sound on computer speaker.

Illustration :

```
#include<stdio.h>
main()
{
   printf("Hello Riti\a");
}
```

When the above program is run, a bell is produced after the string Hello Riti is displayed.

SHORTCUTS IN C

F3	Open(load a file)
F2	Save a file
Alt + X	Quit
Shift + Delete	Cut
Ctrl + Insert	Copy
Shift + Insert	Paste
Ctrl + Del	Clear
Alt + F7	Previous error
Alt + F8	Next error
Ctrl + F9	Run
Ctrl + F2	Program reset
F4	Goto cursor
F7	Step over
F8	Trace into
Alt + F4	Data Inspect
Ctrl + F4	Evaluate/Modify
Ctrl + F3	Call stack
Ctrl + F8	Toggle breakpoint
Ctrl + F5	Size/move
F5	Zoom
F6	Next
Alt + F3	Close
Alt + F5	User screen
Alt + 0 (zero)	Window list
Shift + F1	Index
Ctrl + F1	Topic Search
Alt + F1	Previous topic

❑❑❑

Chapter **2**

Input and Output Functions in C

Generally all the input and output functions of C language revolve around `scanf()` and `printf( )` functions. These functions are explained in details in this chapter. The other input/output functions have been explained in other chapters at appropriate places.

SCANF( ) FUNCTION

Task of the Function

(*i*) It reads one character at a time from standard input unit mostly the keyboard.

(*ii*) It formats each input field according to specification given in the format string.

(*iii*) It stores formatted input in memory location.

The `scanf()` function is available in `stdio.h` header file. All C programs must include preprocessor directive which use `scanf()`.

```
#include <stdio.h>
int scanf(const char format-string [,address,.....]);
```

The format string is a character string that is also called control string. It contains conversion specifications describing the characteristics of the input data.

The addresses are the memory locations of the variables where the input data is stored. The addresses are also called `arguments` of the `scanf` function. The ampersand (&) is called address operator. Every variable except an array is preceded by an address operator (&). Address operator converts a variable into a pointer. A pointer is a memory address of a variable.

`int` has been placed before the function that indicates that `scanf` function will return an integer. It returns the number of successfully assigned input fields. The return value does not include scanned fields which were not stored. When the end of file is reached, it returns `EOF`. If the function reads input fields but no field is stored, it returns 0.

Complete syntax of the format string is as follows :

```
%[width][F|N|h|1/L]  type
```

(*i*) **Percent (%)**

It marks the starting of the format specification. Each format starts with the percent character (%).

(*ii*) **Width Specifier**

It is an optional format string component. It keeps control on the maximum number of character that are inputted from the current input field. It will read less digits if the function encountes a whole space or any unconvertible character.

For example, if 15 10 is entered as 15 10, it will read only 15 and it will not read digits after space.

Similarly 15a10 will be read upto 15 since a is uncountable character as digit.

(*iii*) **Pointer Size Modifier**

`F` and `N` are called optional size modifiers.

(*iv*) **Argument-Type Modifier**

The `h,I,L` are optional argument-type modifiers where `h` indicates short int. The character modifies integer and floating point quantities. If the type is `int`, `I` makes it `long int`. If the type is floating point, `I` specifies it `double`. If the type is floating-point, `L` indicates a `long double`.

(*v*) **Type Conversion Character**

It indicates format specification for input fields. Some of the important data input and output arguments are given below :

Type (Conversion Factor)	*Input*	*Output Argument*
d	Decimal integer	pointer to int
D	Decimal integer	pointer to long
i	Decimal, octal, or hexadecimal integer	pointer to int. integer
I	Decimal, octal, or hexadecimal integer	pointer to long. integer
o	Octal integer	pointer to int
O	Octal integer	pointer to long
u	Unsigned decimal	pointer to unsigned int integer
U	Unsigned decimal	pointer to unsigned long integer
x	Hexadecimal integer	pointer to int
X	Hexadecimal integer	pointer to long
f	Floating point	pointer to float
e	Floating point	pointer to float
g	Floating point	pointer to float
F	Floating point	pointer to double
G	Floating point	pointer to double
c	Character	pointer to a character

s	String pointer	pointer to array of characters
	%character	No conversion, with %% //the second character is stored.
n	none	It stores the number of characters read successfully up to the %n. pointer to `int`.
p	Hexadecimal form	Defaults of the YYYY. pointer size or XXXX.YYYY depending on the (segment.offset) memory model.

The input given to the `scanf()` may be of int, long, float, double, char, array, octal, hexadecimal types.

The `scanf` function gives correct results when there is one to one correspondence between arguments and input format specification fields, If there are more arguments than the format fields, excess arguments will be ignored. If the arguments are less than the format fields, the result will be undefined. Some statements using `scanf` function are given below to illustrate the usage of `scanf` function.

Statement	*Meaning*
1. `scanf("%d", &n);`	It reads one `int` type value and stores it at an address associated with n.
2. `scanf("%d%d%d",` `&n1, &n2, &num);`	It reads three `int` type values and stores them at memory addresses associated with **1, 2, 3.**
3. `scanf("%5d", &num);`	It read not more than digits of `int` type value and stores it at memory address associated with `num`. 5 is a width specifier.
4. `scanf("%c%c%c",` `&ch1, &ch1, &ch1);`	It reads three characters and stores them at memory address associated with `ch1, ch2, ch3` respectively.
5. `scanf("%u",&a);`	It reads an unsigned `int` type number and stores the same at the address associated with `a`.
6. `scanf("%U", &b);`	It reads an unsigned `long` number and stores the same at address associated with `b`.
7. `scanf("%D, &z);` `scanf("%ld", &z);`	It reads is signed `long` number and stores the same at the address associated with `z`.
8. `scanf("%f", &k);`	It reads a floating-point value and stores the same at the address associated with `k`.
9. `scanf("%lf", &j);`	It reads a `double` value and stores the same at the address associated with `j`. Note the use of `if`.
10. `scanf("%s", name);`	The conversion specification %**s** is used for string and array. There is no ampersand before name. The array **name** is a pointer, therefore, it does not need address operator (&).

OPERATION OF SCANF FUNCTION

The `scanf` function is explained for each of the data types.

(*i*) char TYPE

The use of `scanf` function has been explained to input character data with examples which will be supplemented by programs.

Example :

Read three characters SAN.

```
char c1, c2, c3; /* declare the characters */
scanf ("%c%c%c", &c1, &c2, &c3);            /* read the characters */
```

In the above example, conversion specification %c has been used to read a character. White space is also a character.

Program

What does the following program do ? Explain in the light of puts, `scanf` and `printf` functions.

```
#include<stdio.h>
main()
{
   char c1, c2;
   puts("Enter Two characters");
   scanf("%c %c", &c1, &c2);
   puts("Enter Two characters");
   scanf("%c%c" &c1, &c2 );
   printf("%c%c\n", c1, c2);
   printf("%c%c\n", c1, c2);
}
```

Output

```
Enter Two characters
SA
SA
Enter Two characters
SA
S
```

In the above example, the `puts()` function is used to display prompts.

(*i*) The line puts ("Enter Two characters"); displays the string in bracket and shifts the cursor to the next line.

(*ii*) The line `printf ("%c%c\n", c1, c2);`
displays the value of c1 and c2 according to %c specification and shifts the cursor to the next line.

(*iii*) \n is the escape sequence for new line character within the printf function.

(*iv*) There is no need to put \n sequence in the `puts()` function. It already includes its usage and puts the cursor to the next line.

In the second output of the above program, only 'S' is displayed and 'M' is missed.

c1	c2
'S'	'A'
\n	'S'

The second `scanf()` function assigns newline character \n to c1 and 'S' to c2.

Program

In the following brief program, ASCII code of the character is displayed.

```
#include<stdio.h>
main()
{
    char c= 'A';
    printf("ASCII value%c", c);
}
```

Output

```
ASCII value 65
```

`In the above program variable c is declared as type char.`

Final Words about `scanf()` function in reading char type data.

(*i*) All char data types are of int type. Each character has its own ASCII value.

Type	*Range*
signed char	–128 to 127
unsigned char	0 to 255

(*ii*) The c-conversion is used to read a character, d-conversion reads a signed char ASCII code and u-conversion reads an unsigned char ASCII code.

(*ii*) `int Type`

The `int` type may be signed, unsigned `int`, signed and unsigned `long`. The following conversion specifications are used to input `int` type data.

Data Type	*Conversion Specification*
unsigned decimal int	`%u`
signed decimal int	`%d or %i`
unsigned	`long %lu or %U`
long	`%ld or %D or %I`

Program

The following program is based on reading and writing of signed and unsigned numbers (int and long type).

```
#include<stdio.h>
main()
{
    int x,y;
    unsigned un;
    long l;
    puts("Enter one signed and one unsigned int numbers");
    scanf("%d%u", &x, &un);
    printf("signed int=%d unsigned int=%u\n",x, un);
    puts("Enter 5-digit unsigned number");
    scanf("%4u%*c",&un);
    printf("First four digits of this number = %u\n",un);
    printf("Enter two integers separated by any letter\n");
    scanf("%d%*c%d",&x,&y);
    printf("%d%d\n",x,y);
    puts("Enter a long number");
    scanf("%D",&l);
    printf("%ld\n",l);
}
```

Output

```
Enter one signed and one unsigned int numbers
-5432156789
signed int = -54321 unsigned int = 56789
Enter 5-digit unsigned number
56789
First four digits of this number = 5678
Enter two number separated by any letter
567 x 345
567 345
Enter a long number
4567890
4567890
```

Description of the Program

In the above program first `scanf()` statement reads one signed and unsigned numbers using %d and %u conversion.

The next scanf statement *i.e.,* "%4u %*c" uses format for input.

%4u conversion specification reads first four digits of the number.

The %*c ensures that fifth digit should not be read.

Some More Points in Conversion Specifications

(*i*) You can use comma as conversion specification separator.

```
scanf ("%d, %d", &a, &b);
```

The input data will be entered using comma.

123, 234 etc.

(*ii*) You can use embedded characters as conversion specification separators. The output will have the some embedded character.

```
scanf("%dx %dy", &a, &b);
```

The input data will be

123 x 234y

and the output will not change.

(*iii*) **Float and Double Types**

The following conversion specifications are used for scanning float and double data types.

Data Type	*Conversion Specification*
Float	%f
double	%lf
long double	%Lf

Data in an Exponent Form

Float	%e
Float	%g
double	%le or %E or %G
long double	%Le or %Lg

Program

Writing of float and double data type

```
#include<stdio.h>
main()
{
    float x,y;
    double z;
    puts("Enter one floating-point and one double number");
    scanf("f%lf",&x,&z);
    printf("float number=%f\n",x);
    printf("double number=%lf\n",z);
}
```

Output

```
Enter one floating point and one double number
5678.23  5678.23
float number = 5678.22990
double number = 5678.230000
```

The use of scanf( ) function with arrays, structures, pointers etc. has been described in next chapters.

PRINTF( ) FUNCTION

The task of the `printf()` function is just reverse of `scanf()` function. The `printf()` functions writes formatted output to output devices.

General Syntax :

```
%[flags]  [width][.precision]  type
```

The usage of the format specification field shown above, has been mentioned below :

(*i*) `percent(%)`

It indicates the beginning of the conversion specification like in the `scanf` function.

(*ii*) `Flags`

They specify parameters for output justification either left or right, decimal points and signs etc.

(*iii*) `Width`

Width specifier indicates the minimum numbers of characters to print padding left-over places with blanks or zeros.

(*iv*) `Precision`

This specifier specifies the maximum of characters to print for characters and minimum number of digits to print for integers.

(*v*) `Conversion Type Characters`

The `printf` function includes almost all the type characters and input arguments of the `scanf` functions, except a few type characters and input arguments.

Type Character	*Input Argument*	*Output Format*
d	integer	signed decimal int
i	integer	signed decimal int
o	integer	unsigned octal int
x	integer	unsigned hexadecimal int with a through f
X	integer	unsigned hexadecimal int with A through F
f	floating point	signed decimal of the form [-]dd...d.dddddd
e	floating point	signed scientific of the form [-]d.dddd e[+/-]dddd
g	floating point	signed in either e or f form depending on size.
E	floating point	e form with E as exponent
G	floating point	g form with E as exponent
e	Character	single character
s	String pointer	displays characters until NULL or precision is reached.
%	none	% character
n	pointer to int	stores the number of characters displayed.
p	pointer	displays near pointers as YYYY and far pointer as XXXX:YYYY

The `printf` function does not include D, O, I and U types which can be used with the `scanf` function.

USE OF FLAGS

A flag is a series of characters that controls justification of data.

Following characters are enlisted which are used to control justification of data.

Character	*Output Format*
–	Data begins from left with spaces to right.
+	Data begins from right. It will also show the leading sign of + or – with the number depending on the sign of number.
space	Right justified with leading spaces.
#	It indicates alternate form of conversion. It does not affect the data types c, s, d, i, u. In case of type x or X, 0x or 0X will be prefixed. In case of types e, E, or f, the output will contain a decimal point.

In case of g or G, the output will be the same as e and E except the trailing zeroes will not be removed.

Program

```
//Use of flags.
   #include<stdio.h>
   main()
   {
      int x = 3456;
      float y = 456.78;
      printf("Use of flag(-)      %-8d\n",x);      /*line1*/
      printf("Use of flag(+)      %+8d\n",x);      /*line2*/
      printf("Use of flag(space)  %8d\",x);        /*line3*/
      printf("Use of flag(#)      %#8.0f\n",y);    /*line4*/
      printf("Use of flag(#)      %#8.0e\n",y);    /*line5*/
   }
```

Output

```
Use of flag (-)          3456bbbb  (b means blank)
Use of flag (+)          +3456
Use of flag (space)      bbbb3456
Use of flag (#)          457
Use of flag (#)          5.0  +02
```

(Description of the Program)

line 1 : Use of '–' left justifies the data with trailing spaces.

line 2 : Use of '+' prefixes '+' sign along with right justification.

line 3 : Use of space right justifies the data with leading spaces.

line 4 : Use of # with f-format inserts a decimal at the end.

line 5 : Use of # with e-format inserts a decimal at the end.

WIDTH SPECIFIER

In printf() function, three types of width specifiers can be used. It will be clear from the following example :

```
int a = 345;
printf("%2d",a);
printf("%8d",a);
printf("%08d",a);
```

The result will be obtained in the following formats :

Width Specifier	*Output Format*
n(2)	345 If the number of digits are more than the width, all digits are displayed.
n(8)	bbbbb345 If the number of digits are less than the width, the left places are filled with equal blanks.
On(8)	00000345 Here n is the width which is unsigned integer. Here n character (8) will be printed. If output value is less than n (*i.e.,* 8 in the example), the left places are filled with equal zeros.

❑❑❑

Chapter

Data Types in C

INTRODUCTION

To write programs, a programmer must have ample knowledge of data types, variables and constants.

C provides a set of predefined data types.

CONCEPTS OF DATA TYPES

Data used in computer is of various types. It may include integers, characters, strings etc.

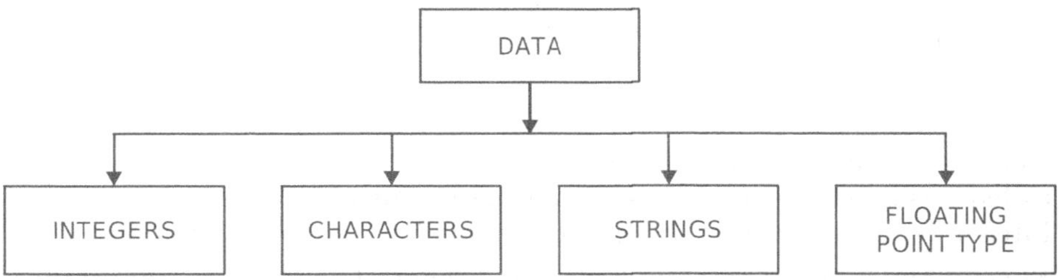

Fig. 3.1

A programmer has to deal with various types of data; therefore, it becomes necessary that the programming language facilitates the programmer in all types of data. The programming language C provides all types of data. Data types can be classified into two categories.

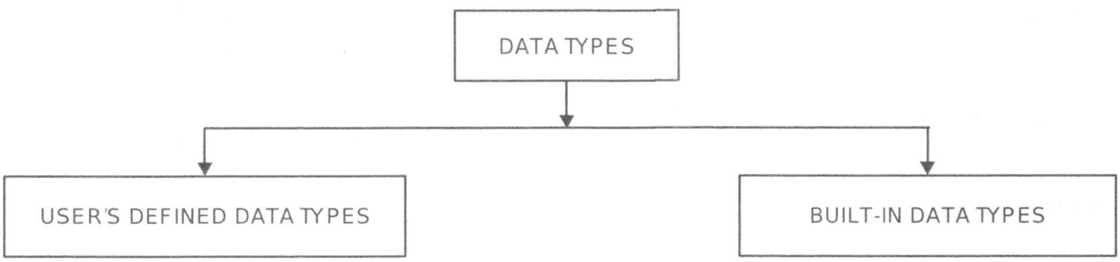

Fig. 3.2

BUILT-IN DATA TYPES

These data types known as standard data types are the part of C language.

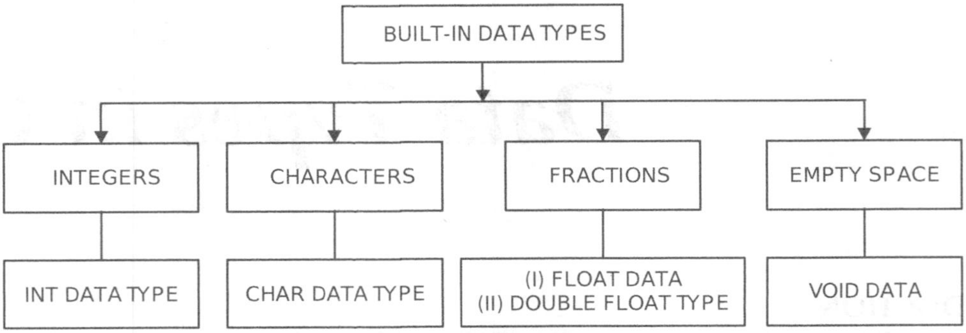

Fig. 3.3

INTEGERS

Integers are whole number such as 3, 10, 20, –5, –12, etc. No fractional part is used in integers. Integers are generally constants. Range of values is -2^{15} to $2^{15} - 1$ (*i.e.,*–32768 to 32767).

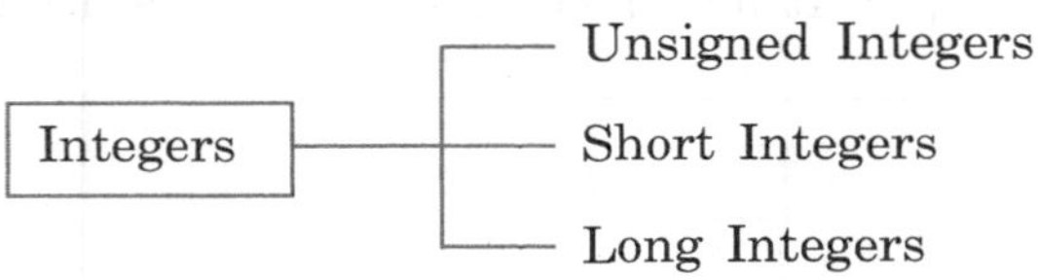

(*i*) *Unsigned Integers.* Those non-negative whose value varies from 0 to 65535, are called unsigned integers. If we have to use value of 32770, we have to use unsigned integer because ordinary integer can provide a value to a maximum of 32767.

(*ii*) *Short Integers.* Short integers have small range of value. The value of these integers varies between –128 to 127. This type of integers takes lesser space for storage.

(*iii*) *Long Integers.* Long integers have wide range of values. The value varies between –429467296 to 329467295.

Data Types	*Size Bits*	*Range*
Integer	16 Bits	-2^{15} to $2^{15} -1$ (–32768 to 32767)
Unsigned Integer	16 Bits	0 to $2^{16} -1$ (0 to 65535)
Short Integer	8 Bits	-2^{7} to $2^{7} -1$ (–128 to 127)
Long Integer	32 Bits	-2^{32} to $2^{32} -1$ (–4294967296 to 4294967295)

Character Types

Character (char) types are one byte in size and a character constant varies between 0 to 255. The characters are stored in the computer memory as integers in Binary Form. Each character is assigned a particular value according to ASCII codes [ASCII means—American Standard Code for Information Interchange]. It is worth noting that no computer language can use more than 256 characters [A to Z, numbers, punctuation marks etc.], therefore, these characters are assigned coding from 0–255.

Character Types	*Size*	*Range*
char	1 Byte	-2^7 to $2^7 -1$ (–128 to 127)
unsigned char	1 Byte	0 to $2^8 -1$ (0 to 255)
signed char	1 Byte	-2^7 to $2^7 -1$ (–128 to 127)

SPECIAL PRINTING CHARACTERS

Characters can be written by writing the character in single quotes. But some characters are written in C program by using Escape, Carriage Return. Tab characters. C compiler recognizes these characters for formatting.

Escape character (\) changes the meaning of the character which follows it, *e.g.,* the character b indicates the letter b but when it is preceded by escape character, it means Back Space.

Character	*Meaning*
`\n`	New Line
`\t`	Horizontal Tab
`\v`	Vertical Tab
`\b`	Back Space
`\\`	Back Slash
`\"`	Double Quotes
`\'`	Single Quote
`\?`	Question Mark

String

String is a series of characters. A string is enclosed within double quotes. A string is used to write or store messages.

"GOOD MORNING"

The "GOOD MORNING" is a string and the characters of a string are stored in sequential locations.

GOOD MORNING ϕ

└──→ Null Character

The null character is added at the end of the string automatically by the compiler.

Floating Point Constants

A fractional number is a floating point number. Decimal in a number means that the number is a floating number.

A floating point constant may have +ve or –ve sign. If it has no sign, the number is treated as positive. Floating form provides greater range of integers between –ve to +ve.

Type	*Size*	*Range*
float	4 Bytes	3.4×10^{-38} to 3.4×10^{38}
double	8 Bytes	1.7×10^{-308} to 1.7×10^{308}
long double	10 Bytes	3.4×10^{-4932} to 3.4×10^{4932}

Some Valid Floating Point Constants

(*i*) 10.0 (with decimal)

(*ii*) +0.1234 (with + ve sign)

(*iii*) –12.18 (with – ve sign)

Invalid Floating Point Constants

(*i*) 1234 (Decimal missing)

(*ii*) 12. (Fractional portion is absent)

(*iii*) ± 12.123 (Both signs not allowed)

(*iv*) + 12.123 (Blank space after + sign not allowed)

(*v*) – 12.123 (Blank space after – sign not allowed)

(*vi*) 12,23.1516 (Comma not allowed)

(*vii*) 12,23.1516 (Blank space between digits not allowed)

The range of floating-point constants can be written in terms of power having base 10.

Floating-point constants written in this form are called to be in exponent form (E-notation). This notation is also called standard form.

12340000 → 1.234×10^{6}

0.1234 → 1.234×10^{-1} Standard Form

0.00001234 → 1.234×10^{-5} Scientific Notation

Representation in Exponent form in C

9.136×10^{6} can be written as 9.136E6

9.136×10^{-6} can be written as 9.136E–6

9.136×10^{6} can be written as 9.136E+6

9.136×10^{6} can also be written as 9.136E06

E

Left Part Right Part

Left Part is called mantissa and right part is exponent.

9.136E is invalid notation because exponent is absent.

E6 is invalid notation because mantissa is absent.

Double Data Type occupies double memory than that of float types. This stores floating point number with much larger range.

USER DEFINED DATA TYPES

User has the facility in the programming language to create data types according to his own needs. Not only he can use built-in data types but also data types as per his own needs. These types contain array, function, pointers, constants, classes structures etc.

Array

An array is a collection of fixed-size finite number of objects, data value that belong to the same type. An array is a collection of data storage locations. Each of the locations holds same type of Data. The Storage Location is called an element or component of the array. The individual element within the array is called **subscript.**

The subscript is the number of elements in the array surrounded by square brackets [ ].

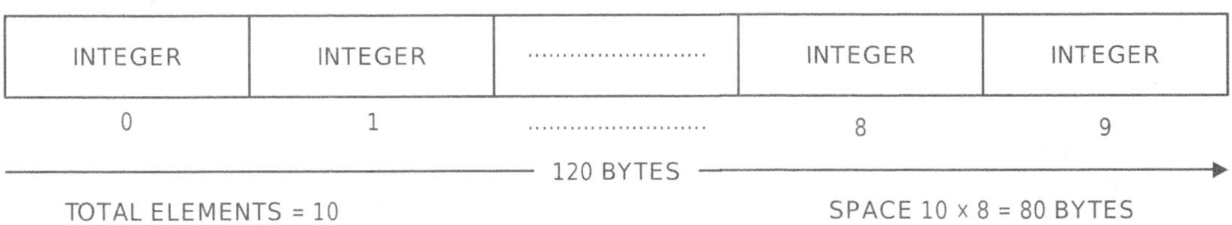

(DECLARING AN ARRAY)

Fig. 3.4

Array elements are counted beginning with 0.

In the above figure 10. elements are numbered from [0] to [19]

An array may be one-dimensional, two-dimensional or multi-dimensional depending upon the specification of elements.

Pointer

A pointer is a variable that holds a memory address within.

Each variable is located at a particular position in the memory which is known as **address.** The address can be stored in a pointer. A program accesses the value in the address stored in the pointer by using indirection operator.

General Syntax

```
type* ptr;
```

(ptr is the name of pointer)

In program, pointers are used for the following tasks :

(*i*) Managing data on free storage locations of the memory.

(*ii*) Passing variables by reference to functions.

(*iii*) Accessing class member data and functions.

Function

A function is a subprogram that acts on data and returns a value. A function can be invoked from the other parts of the program.

Every C program contains one function, *i.e.,* `main()`. When the program starts, `main()` automatically becomes active and can call other functions. A function can perform a specific task for the programmer. It is better to use multiple functions in the lengthy programs.

Functions are of Two Types :

(*i*) Built-in functions

(*ii*) User-defined functions.

The concept of functions has been discussed in details in a separate chapter.

Illustration

This program Illustrates the use of a function.

```
#include<stdio.h>
   float square(float);      //Function declaration
   main()
   {
      clrscr();
      float number;
      puts("Enter Number");
      scanf("%f", &number);
      printf("square is = "%f",square(number));
      return 0;
   }
   float square (float x)
   {
      return x*x;
   }
```

Reference

A reference is an alias, *i.e.,* an alternative name for an object. As soon as a reference is created, the program initializes it with the name of previously defined object. This object is called **target.** Any change (s) made in the reference directly affects/affect the Target.

General Syntax :

type &someRef = somevariable;

some Ref is a reference to the variable that is initialized to refer to somevariable.

Variable

A variable is a quantity which can change during a program execution. In C, a variable is a location where the information is stored. This location exists in computer memory where the value/information can be stored and in case of need it can be retrieved. Depending upon the size, a variable, it can occupy one or more memory address.

Variables can be created by any combination of letters without spaces. Variables name may be short or descriptive but a descriptive variable name makes it easier to understand the flow of the program. Some keywords are reserved in C and cannot be used as variable name like–if, while, main, for. We can create more than one variable of the same type in a single statement. This can be done by the following syntax :

Syntax :

```
type varname, VarName;
```

Rules for Creating Variables

1. A variable may consist one or more than one letters, numerals and underscore (_).
2. The first letter of the variable name cannot be a numeral. It can be any letter or underscore.
3. Do not use keywords as variable names.
4. Obtain the list of reserved keywords. A keyword cannot be used as variable name.
5. No blank space is allowed in a variable name.
6. C is a case sensitive language. It can distinguish between uppercase and lowercase letters.

Kalyani	KALYANI	KaLyAni
kAlyani	KALYaNi	

All these are different variables.

7. Use of any special character is not allowed in the variable name.

KAL* + NI is invalid variable name.

8. Try to use the same style of using the variable names throughout the program.

Declaration of Variables

Declaration of variable about its data type is using essential before using it in a C programme. If declaration is not done, error message will appear in the programme.

Variable may be built-in-data type or user-defined type. A variable name is an identifier and all rules pertaining to identifiers apply on the variables.

General Syntax of Declaration :

data-type list;

Following are some examples of valid declaration of variables :

1. int value;
2. double salary, bonus, increment;
3. int principle, rate, time;
4. unsigned long int number, cube;

5. unsigned short int odd;
6. float a, sum;

It is clear from the above examples that when two or more identifiers belong to the same data type, we can use single declaration statement. Identifiers are separated by comma. The main advantage of declaration of variables is that the programmer is not at compulsion to trace back the beginning of the program to ascertain the data type linked with these identifiers. A variable can be declared anywhere in the program.

The following are valid variable declarations :

1. int age;
   age = 15;
2. int weight;
   weight = 50;
3. int height;
   int age;
   int weight;
   height = 165;
   age = 15;
   weight = 50;

Illustration

The following program illustrates that a variable can be declared anywhere in the program.

```
#include<stdio.h>
void main()
{
    int a, b;
    a = 15;
    b = 25;
    int c;
    c = a + b;        //declaration of variable at new place
    printf("sum of numbers is =%d",c);
    return 0;
}
```

How to Assign a Value to a Variable ?

The value to a variable can be assigned using = sign. This equal sign is called Assignment operator.

Look at the following program segment :

Program

```
main()
{
    int length;
```

```
    int breadth;
    int height;
    length = 12;  //Assign the value to length
    breadth = 8;  //Assign the value to breadth
    height = 6;   //Assign the value to height
}
```

Declaring Multiple Variables

You can declare multiple variables within C programs. You have to tell the variable name and its type to the C compiler.

Look at these statements

int length;

int breadth;

int height;

These variables are of same type int. When the variables are of same type, you can declare them in a single line. The above three statements can be declared as

int length, breadth, height;

Each variable name is separated by comma.

THE ACCESS MODIFIER CONSTANT

Constant are frequently used in C programs. Sometimes a constant is used a number of times and if any change is to be made in the value, it becomes a cumbersome job for the programmer. If some meaningful name is given to the constant and suitable value is assigned, the job becomes easy. In case the value of the constant is changed, it is required to change this value only in the definition of constant and not at other places.

const data-type name = value;

Let us differentiate between the following declarations :

intvalue = 25; and const intvalue 25;

The first statement declares a variable `value` with initial value being 25. This can be changed in the program.

In the second statement the variable `value` becomes constant and cannot be changed in the program. Here keyword `const` is an access modifier for variables.

❑❑❑

Chapter

Operators and Expressions in C

OPERATORS

An operator may be a symbol or letter which causes the compiler to take an action and produce a value. An operator acts on different data items that are called **Operands.**

For example

a + b is an expression in which sign + is an operator which specifies the operation of addition. Similarly a * b is an expression in which * operator specifies the operation of multiplication.

TYPES OF OPERATORS

Operators are of following types :

(*i*) Arithmetical Operators

(*ii*) Increment Decrement Operators

(*iii*) Binary Operators

(*iv*) Logical Operators

(*v*) Conditional Operators

Arithmetical Operators

For various mathematical calculations arithmetical operators are used. The result of an arithmetical expression is a numerical value. An arithmetical expression may be a variable or a constant or a combination of both. Variables or functions are connected with arithmetical operators.

Arithmetical operators are of two types :

(*i*) Unary Arithmetic Operator

(*ii*) Binary Arithmetic Operator.

Unary Arithmetic Operator

The operator unary needs only one operand. It may be either + or –.

For example $-x$, $+b$ use unary operator which are negative and positive respectively.

(*a*) *Unary+ :* The unary + operator should have arithmetic type. The result comes in the value or argument.

if x = 30	then	+ x means 30
		x means + 30
	and	+ x means + 30
if x = – 30	then	+ x means – 30

(*b*) *Unary – :* The unary – operator should have arithmetic type. The result comes in negative.

if x = – 30	then	– x means 30
		– x means – 30

Binary Arithmetic Operators

The Binary Arithmetic Operators act upon two operands. The following arithmetical operators require two operands.

Symbols	*Meaning*	*Example*
+	Addition	a + b
–	Subtraction	a - b
*	Multiplication	a * b
/	Slash or Division	a/b
%	Modulus or Remainder	a % b

Brief Explanation

(*i*) *Addition Operator :* Addition operator adds two values of operands.

For example,

a + b	If	a = 20
	and	b = 30

then a + b = 50

The result obtained is 50 which is sum of the values of two operands.

(*ii*) *Subtraction Operator :* The subtraction operator-subtracts two values of operands.

For example,

a – b	if	a = 30
		b = 19
then		a – b = 11

The result obtained is subtraction of values of two operands.

(*iii*) *Multiplication Operator :* The multiplication operator * multiplies the values of operands.

For example,

if	a = 8
	b = 9

then a * b = 72

Here the result obtained is multiplication of two values of operands.

(*iv*) *Division Operator :* The division operator/divides the first operand by the second.

For example,

if a = 60

b = 5

a/b = 12

(*v*) *Modulus Operator :* The modulus operator % obtains the remainder when first operand is divided by the second.

For example,

if a = 25

b = 6

a%b = 1

Increment and Decrement Operator

C provides special operators + + and – – operators which are not provided by many other high level languages. These operators are called increment and decrement operators.

The increment operators + + adds 1 to its operand.

+ + a means a + 1 a + + means a + 1

and – – a means a – 1 a – – means a – 1

But these operators exist in 2 types.

(*i*) Prefix

(*ii*) Postfix

Prefix notation before its operand and postfix notation after its operand.

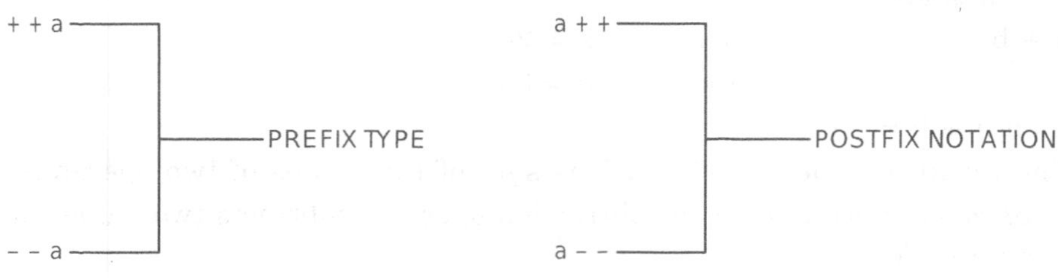

Fig. 4.1

Prefix increment or decrement operators (like + + a and – – a) follow the rule :

FIRST CHANGE AND USE. These operators first change the value of their operand and then use a new value in the expression.

For example take the following expressions :

1. a = + + i * 10; where i = 10

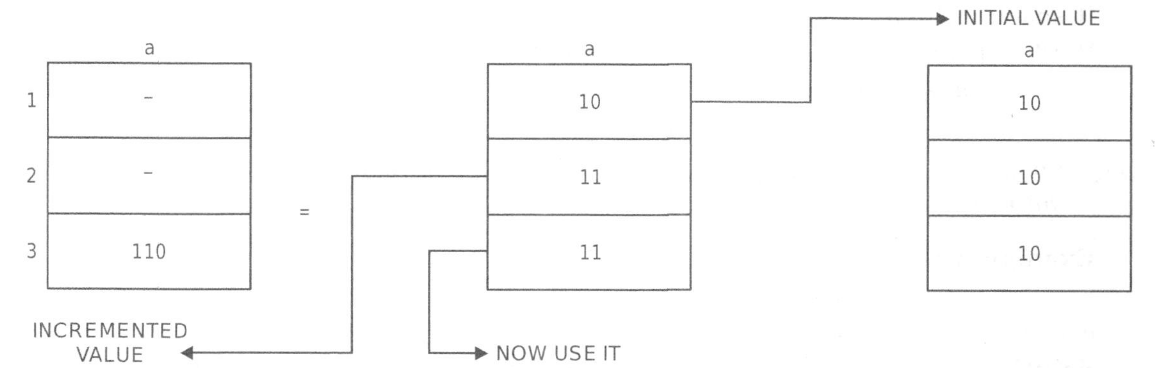

Fig. 4.2

Postfix increment or decrement operators follow the rule : **FIRST USE AND THEN CHANGE.** They first use the same value and then increment and decrement the value and use it in the expression.

For example

a = a + + * 10;   where i = 10

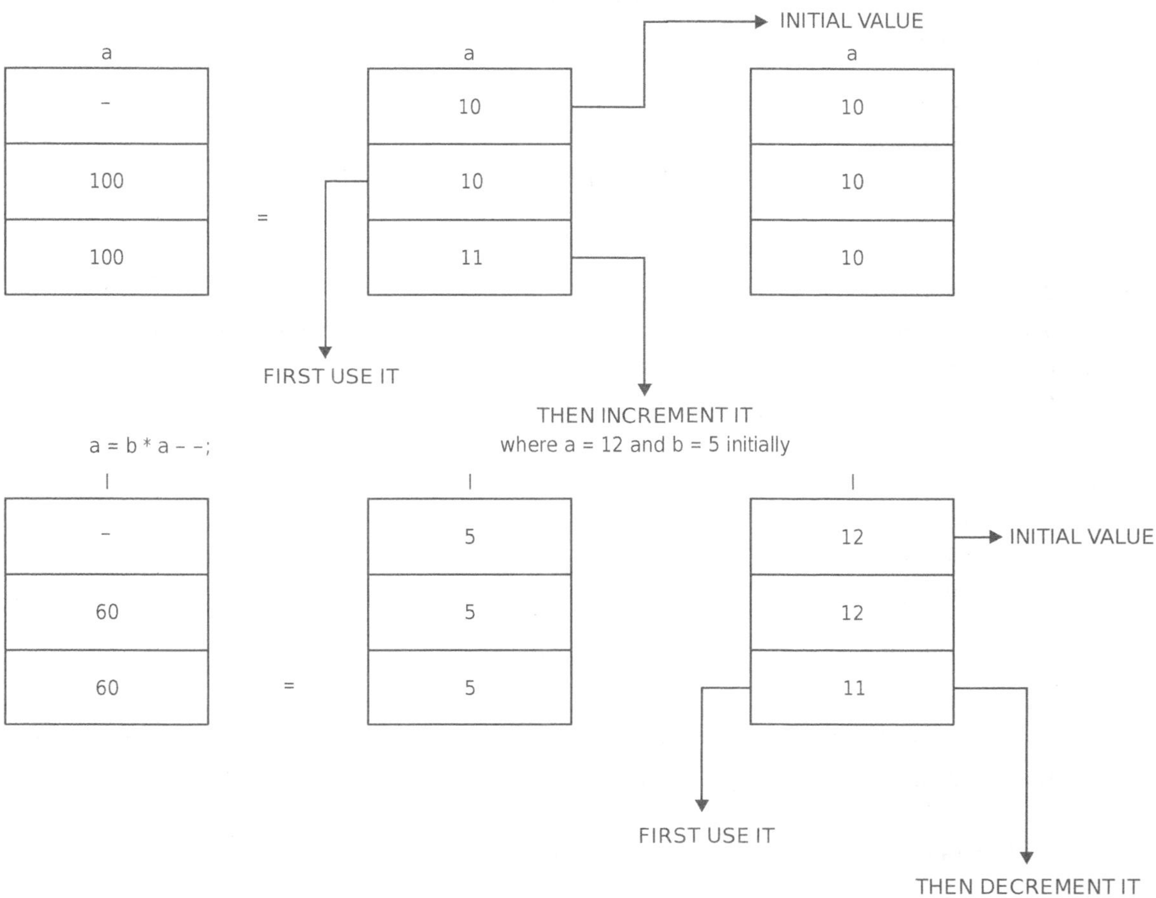

Fig. 4.3

It should be kept in mind that + + and – – operators operate on a single operand.

Postfix operators have high precedence over prefix operators.

a + + has high precedence over + + a

a – – has high precedence over – – a

Note: *When the + + and – – operators are used in expressions instead of single operand, they produce different results.*

Example : *Evaluate*

a = b + + + b;

where *b = 15*

Solution. Since + + b is prefix unary operator. It has higher precedence over b. The rule is **First change and then use.** + + b will be 15 + 1 = 16.

Now incremented value will be used in the expression.

a = 16 + 16 = 32

Examples :

1. *Use of Prefix Increment Operator*

   Consider the following program segment

```
........................
........................
a = 10;
netvalue = ++ a*8;
printf ("net value = %d", netvalue);
........................
........................
```

   The output will be

   netvalue = 88 i.e., (11 × 8) *(First increment the value)*

2. *Use of Postfix Increment Operator*

   Consider the following program segment

```
........................
........................
a = 10;
netvalue = i ++ *8;
printf("net value =", netvalue);
........................
```

   The output of that program will be

   a = 20;

   net value = 80 i.e., (10 × 8) *(First use the value)*

3. *Evaluate the following expressions (Given a = 15, b = 10)*

   (i) a% b++ *(ii) ++a – b – –*

   (iii) a++– b–– *(iv) a––+ b ++*

Solution :

(*i*) 15% (10 + +) = 15% 10 = 5

(*ii*) + + 15 – (0 – –) = 16 – 10 = 6

(*iii*) 15 + + – (10 – –) = 15 – 10 = 5

(*iv*) 15 – – + (10 + +) = 15 + 10 = 25

Relational Operators

Relational operators are frequently used in the programs.

Relational operators are used to establish the relationship between different operands. These are used for comparison also. There are two mathematical expressions and these are connected by a relational operator. The relational expression returns 0 if the relation is false and returns 1 if the relation is true. Relational operators are shown in the following table.

Symbol	*Meaning*
>	Greater than
<	Less than
> =	Greater than, equal to
< =	Less than, equal to
= =	Equal to
! =	Not Equal to

The following table will help you understanding the relational operators and their results

a	*b*	*a>b*	*a<b*	*a>=b*	*a<=b*	*a= =b*	*a!=b*
1	0	1	0	1	0	0	1
0	1	0	1	0	1	0	1
1	1	0	0	1	1	1	0

In the above table, the right part of table contains Os and Is.

0 means false.

1 means true.

Example 1. *If x = 10 and y = 5; evaluate the following expressions.*

1. *x! = y*
2. *x<y*
3. *x+y<y*

Solution :

1. The expression results into true because *x* = 10 and *y* = 5. These value are not equal. We get the value 1 which means the expression is true.
2. The expression is true because the value of *x* is greater than *y*. Result is 0 (false).
3. The expression is false because the value of *x* + *y* = 10 + 5 = 15. It is greater than *y*. The result is 0 (false).

Logical Operators

Logical operators are used to combine the results of two or more than two expressions. The method of connecting relationship in these expressions refers as logic and the expressions are called logical expressions.

The logical expression returns 1 if the results is true otherwise 0.

C provides the following three logical operators which are listed below :

Symbol	*Meaning*
!	Logical negation (Logical inverse)
||	Logical OR
&&	Logical AND

Logical Operators !

The logical operator (!) has logical negation. It has higher precedence over the remaining logical operators. This operator is also referred to as logical NOT operator. This works on single operand and can be referred to as unary operator. To negate an expression, the expression should be enclosed in parentheses.

The ! operator negates the actual value of the expression. If the expression is true, it becomes false and if the expression is false, it becomes true.

⇒ If the expression is a Zero, ! expression is 1

and if the expression is non-zero, ! expression is 0.

Example :

! (25) is a non-zero expression but it results into 0 (false)

! (20>8) is a true expression because 20>8, but it results into 0 (false).

The Logical OR (||)

The logical OR expression (||) combines two expressions. If both the operands are false, the logical OR operation is false. The logical OR expression results into 1 (true) if either of the operands is true.

Operand 1	*Operand 2*	*Result*
False	False	0 (zero)
True	True	1 (non-zero)
False	True	1 (non-zero)
True	False	1 (non-zero)

The Logical Operator AND (&&)

The logical OR operator (&&) connects two expressions and makes them a single expression. If both the original expressions are true, the resulting expression results a value 1 (true) otherwise false.

Operand 1	*Operand 2*	*Result*
False	False	False
True	True	True
False	True	False
True	False	False

a	*b*	*a&&b*
0	0	0
1	1	1
0	1	0
1	0	0

Examples :

(9 = = 6) && (9 = = 9) It results into 0 (false) because the first expression is false.

(6 = = 6) && (9 = = 9) It results into 1 (true) because both the expression are true.

35 > 49 && 16 > 2 It results into 0 (false) because the first expression is false.

Conditional Operator

C provides a special ternary operator.

Conditional Operator is also called ternary operator. It is represented by (?:). This is the only operator in C which takes three terms (Operands) and returns a value. The value of an expression using this operator is the value of either its second operand or third operand, depending upon the value of first operand. However, ternary operator is sometimes a confused control structure.

(expression1) ? (expression 2) : (expression 3);

If expression 1 is true, the result of the operator is the value of expression 2 ; otherwise it results in the value of expression 3.

The first operand is a test condition, the second and the third operands represent the final value of the expression and out of these values, one is selected.

Example :

```
if a = 5;
    b = 10;
x = (a < b) ? a:b;
```

The above statement reads if *a* is less than *b*, than output the value of *a* otherwise *b*;
The result of the above program segment will be 5.

PRECEDENCE OF OPERATORS

Operators have two main properties of precedence and associativity.

Precedence means the order in which a program performs/evaluates the operations in a formula. All operators have their precedence value. An operator with higher precedence value is evaluated first thereafter the operator having lower precedence value. Multiplication has higher precedence than addition.

Consider the following expression

x = 25 + 4 * 6;

The value of this expression is 49 and not 174. Multiplication takes first place in this expression. The operand 4 is bound with multiplication operator rather. Grouping of operands with operators, occur in two manners.

(*i*) left to right manner (associativity)

(*ii*) right to left manner (associativity)

Left to right associativity means that evaluation is performed from left to right. The compiler starts from the left side. Similarly, right to left associativity means the evaluation from right to left.

When two mathematical operators have the same precedence, they are performed in left to right manner.

x = 2 + 3 + 4 + 5 + 6 * 7 + 8 * 9;

The operation starts from multiplication in the following manner.

x = 2 + 3 + 20 + 42 + 72;

Now the addition operator starts from left to right.

x = 5 + 20 + 42 + 72;

x = 25 + 42 + 72;

x = 67 + 72;

x = 139;

All assignment operators are evaluated in right to left order. The order of precedence can be changed by using parentheses in the expression.

The variables/items in the expression within parentheses are evaluated first than any of the other mathematical operators.

Operator Precedence

Operator	*Associativity*	
() [ ] →	Left to Right	Highest Precedence ↑
+ + − −	Left to Right	
* → *	Left to Right	
* / %	Left to Right	
+ −	Left to Right	
< < > >	Left to Right	

<table>
<tr><td>< < = > > =</td><td>Left to Right</td><td></td></tr>
<tr><td>= = ! =</td><td>Left to Right</td><td></td></tr>
<tr><td>&</td><td>Left to Right</td><td></td></tr>
<tr><td>|</td><td>Left to Right</td><td></td></tr>
<tr><td>& &</td><td>Left to Right</td><td></td></tr>
<tr><td>| |</td><td>Left to Right</td><td></td></tr>
<tr><td>?:</td><td>Right to Left</td><td></td></tr>
<tr><td>= * = / = % =</td><td>Right to Left</td><td></td></tr>
<tr><td>+ = – = & = ^ =</td><td>Right to Left</td><td></td></tr>
<tr><td>| = < < = > > =</td><td>Right to Left</td><td>Lower Precedence</td></tr>
</table>

EXPRESSIONS

An expression means a statement which consists one or more operands and returns a value. It may be combination of operators, variables and constants.

The expression may be simple or complex.

For example

a = b + c ; is an expression which adds two variables b and c.

a = b * c; multiplies two variables b and c.

TYPES OF EXPRESSIONS

There are mainly three types of expression we deal in C.

1. Constant Expressions
2. Integral Expressions
3. Logical Expressions

Constant Expressions

Constant expression consists only constant values.

The following are constant expressions.

20

20 * 6 + 72/2.0

Integral Expressions

Integral Expressions are formed by connecting integer constants using arithmetic operators.

For Example

```
const count = 20;
int a, b, c;
```

(i) a
(ii) b
(iii) a – b
(iv) a + b – c
(v) a + b
(vi) a/b
(vii) a % b
(viii) a * b * c
(ix) a – b + c etc.

Logical Expression

Logical Expressions are those expressions which result into true or false value. They return 0 or 1 value.

0 means false

1 means true

The following are the examples of logical expressions

(i) a > b

(ii) (a + b) > = (a + b – c)

(iii) (a + c) < = ! b

TYPE CONVERSION

The process of converting one type of expressions into another type is called conversion.

There are two types of conversion in C.

1. Implicit (Automatic) Conversion
2. Explicit Conversion

Implicit Conversion

Data types can be mixed in expressions.

For example

x = 25.0/4.5;

is a valid C expression.

When data types are mixed in an expression, the conversion is performed automatically. This process of automatic conversion is called implicit conversion.

This conversion is performed without the intervention of the programmer.

Rules for Implicit Conversion

1. If one of the two operands is of type long double, the other is also converted to a long double.
2. Otherwise, if one of the operands is of type double, the other is converted to double.
3. Otherwise, if one of the operand is float, the other is converted to a float.

4. Otherwise, if one of the operand is unsigned long, the other is converted into unsigned long.
5. Otherwise, if one of the operand is unsigned long, the other is converted into long int.

Explicit Expressions

Explicit expressions are user-defined expressions. C provides type casting facility. The expression can be converted into a specific type.

Type casting is done by using the following syntax.

```
(type) expression;
```

Type casting can be done on the right side of the assignment statement.

Example : Consider the following program segment:

```
................
................
double a;
double b;
double m;
m = a * b;
................
................
```

The multiplication (*) is removed when the result is performed. m is assigned the multiplied value. We can also evaluate a * b after converting it to a double expression.

```
m = (double) a/b;
```

ASSIGNMENT STATEMENT

The assignment operator is represented by symbol '='. The Assignment operator takes the value on the right and stores it in the variable on the left side. An expression is composed of one or more operations. An expression itself has a value, which is same value that is assigned to the left hand operand. The assignment operator has right-to-left associativity. In C programs, the value to a variable can be assigned by = sign. This equal sign is called Assignment operator. Assignment statements can be simple to compound.

The following are the valid simple assignment statements :

```
x = 10;
a = a + 5;
a = b + 10;
```

Let us have a look on various operators made from assignment operator :

=	Assignment
+ =	Addition Assignment
– =	Subtraction Assignment
* =	Multiplication Assignment
/ =	Division Assignment
% =	Remainder Assignment
& =	Bitwise AND Assignment
^ =	Bitwise XOR Assignment
| =	Bitwise OR Assignment
<< =	Bitwise shift left Assignment
>> =	Bitwise shift right Assignment

Compound Assignment statements use the following assignment operators :

* =
/ =
% =
+ =
/ =

The following are the valid expression :

a + = b (equivalent to a = a + b)
a – = b (equivalent to a = a – b)
a * = b (equivalent to a = a * b)
a/ = b (equivalent to a = a/b)
a % = b (equivalent to a = a %b)

VARIABLE INITIALIZATION

In C, a variable is a location to store information. The program can retrieve the value from memory location when required. Any variable in C program can be initialized. The process of initialization is performed with the help of assignment statement. This initialization is of two types.

(*i*) Explicit initialization
(*ii*) Implicit initialization

Explicit Initialization

Explicit initialization uses an assignment operator.

For example

int value = 120;

The initial value of the integer variable value is 120.

Implicit Initialization

In implicit initialization the initial value of the variable is placed within parentheses.

C SHORTHANDS

C provides shorthands to simplify the coding of a certain type of a assignment statement.

For example

a = a + 10; can be written as

a + = 10;

The operator + = instructs the compiler for assigning the value of a + 10 to a. General form of C shorthand.

var = var **operator** expression;

which is same as

var **operator** = expression;

Examples of C shorthand :

x* = 16; is equivalent to x = x* 16;

x/ = 16; is equivalent to x = x/16;

x% = y is equivalent to x = x%y

MORE WORKED-OUT EXAMPLES

Example 1. *What will be the output of the following program ?*

```
#include<stdio.h>
void main()
{
    int x, y, z;
    x = 1;
    y = 9;
    z = 20;
    a = +z+++y+x;
}
```

Solution :

The output will be 21

+z means z *i.e.,* 20

++y means y + 1 *i.e.,* 10

⇒ 20 + 10 + 1 = 31

Example 2. *Write the output of the following :*

```
#include<stdio.h>
void main()
{
    int a = 175;
    a%=15;
    printf("a = %d",a);
}
```

Solution :

The output will be 10

(175 divided by 15, leaves a remainder of 10)

Example 3. *What will be the output of the following program ?*

```
#include<stdio.h>
main()
{
    int x = 20<25;
    printf ("x = %d", x);
}
```

Solution :

The output will be x = 1

(since 25>20, therefore, output will be 1 *i.e.,* True)

Example 4. *What will be the output of following program ?*

```
#include<stdio.h>
main()
{
    int a=0,b=30,c=40;
    a=--b+c+ ++b;
    printf("a=%d",a);
}
```

Solution :

The output will be 100

(a = 29 + 40 + 31 = 100)

Example 5. *Write a program which multiplies two variables with prefix increment operators.*

Solution :

```
//This program obtains the value of multiplication to two
//variables with prefix incremental operators.
#include<stdio.h>
main()
{
    int product;
    int x=11;
    int y=24;
```

```
    puts("Print the value of product with prefix");
    product = (++x) * (++y); //prefix incremental operators
    printf("The product is =%d\n",product);
    return 0;
}
```

The output of the program will be 300.

Example 6. *Write a program which multiplies two variables with postfix increment operators.*

Solution :

```
//This program obtains the value of multiplication of two
//variables with postfix incremental operators.
#include<stdio.h>
main()
{
    int product;
    int x=32;
    int y=10;
    puts("Print the value of product with prefix");
    product = (x++) * (y++); //postfix incremental operators
    printf("The product is =%d\n",product);
    return 0;
}
```

The output of the program will be 320.

❑❑❑

Chapter

I/O Functions

INTRODUCTION

Input/Output (I/O) functions are not directly performed by C. These are the header files which help in performing input/output functions.

C provides a large variety of functions to deal with characters and input/output operations.

These function are mentioned below :

1. `getchar()`
2. `putchar()`
3. `gets()`
4. `puts()`

These functions are also called unformatted console I/O functions.

In C programming the keyboardz is a standard input device and the monitor is a standard output device.

STANDARD DEVICES IN C

Description	*C Name*
Keyboard	stdin
Screen	stdout
Printer	stdprn
Standard auxilary	stdaux
Error Message	stderr

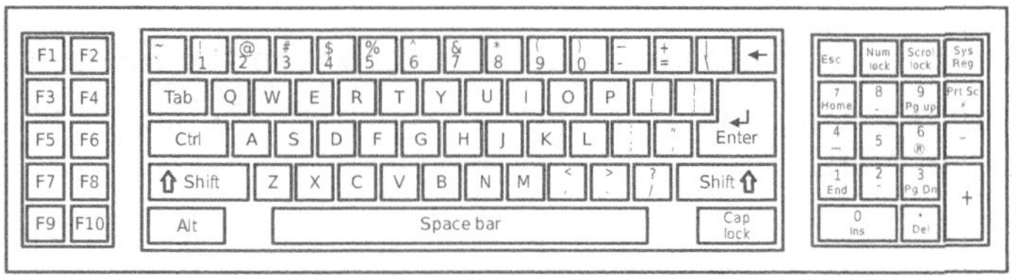

KEY BOARD (stdin)

V.D.U. (stdout)

FLOPPY DISK (stdaux)

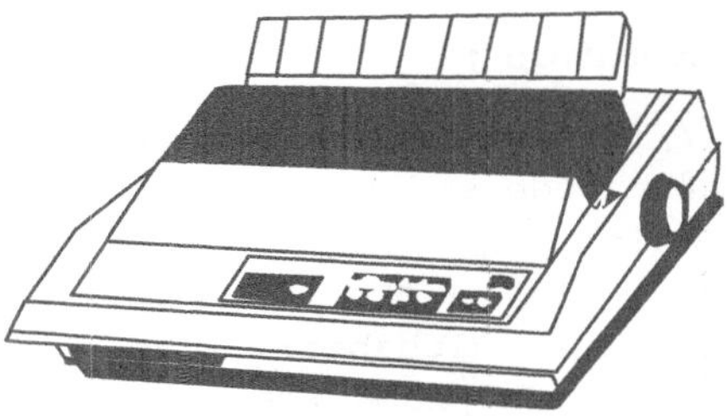

PRINTER (stdprn)

Fig. 5.1

CHARACTER FUNCTIONS getchar( ) AND putchar( )

These functions are based on characters for input and output operations.

getchar( )

The function get char is included in `stdio.h` header file.

The function `getchar()` reads a single character from the standard input device that is usually a keyboard.

It must be noted when getchar is used, the execution of the program is temporarily suspended. When the character is typed by the user from the Keyboard, then this character is communicated to the program. The suspended execution starts again. No argument/s is/are required in the function because getchar function reads a simple character in a given time.

```
..................
..................
char ch;
.................
ch = getchar();
..................
..................
```

putchar( )

The `putchar()` function is used to send a single character (write or display) on the monitor.

Argument is used in this function. When putchar function is executed, the character related with the argument is displayed on VDU screen.

Syntax of `putchar()` function.

putchar(c); where c is any agrument.

The function `putchar()` is also included in stdio.h header file.

Illustration 1. *Write a C program which demonstrates the use of putchar function.*

Solution :

```
//This program illustrates the use of putchar function.
#include<stdio.h>
main()
{
    char alphabet;
    for(alphabet='a';alphabet<='z', alphabet++)
    putchar(alphabet);
}
```

IIlustration 2. *Write a C program which demonstrates the use of getchar() and putchar() functions.*

Solution :

```
//This program illustrates the use of getchar and putchar functions
#include<stdio.h>
main()
{
    char C;
    c=getchar();
    while(c!='@')
    putchar(c);
    c=getchar();
    return0;
}
```

IIlustration 3. *Write a small C program which illustrates the use of getchar( )*

Solution :

```
//This program illustrates the use of getchar function.
#include<stdio.h>
main()
{
    char Character;
    printf("Enter the character:");
    character=getchar();
    if(character==' ')
```

```
        printf("It is a Blank space");
        else
        printf("It is a character");
    }
```

The gets( ) and puts( ) Functions

The function gets() and puts() are string functions which are commonly used to handle character strings. These functions are contained in stdio.h header file.

The gets( ) Function

This function reads a string from the input device, *i.e.,* keyboard.

General Syntax :

gets(string);

This is an unformatted function. As soon as the command of gets() is encountered, the program temporarily stops and restarts as and when the user enters the characters of the string. It is advisable to use **fflush (stdin)** in the program to avoid any interference.

The puts( ) Function

This function puts string or sends string to the output device or to the monitor.

General Syntax :

puts(string;)

String may be any argument. Once the program is executed, message is displayed on the monitor.

Illustration 4. *Develop a C program which illustrates the use of gets() and puts() functions.*

Solution :

```
//This program illustrates the use of gets and puts functions.
#include<stdio.h>
main()
{
    char name[];
    puts("Enter publisher name.");    //reads the size of string
    name=getchar();
    fflush(stdin);                    //clear input buffer.
    puts(name);
    return 0;
}
```

getc( ) and putc( ) Functions

These functions are also character based functions. The `gets()` and `putc()` functions work on files. These functions are capable of reading and writing data from standard input and output devices by stdin and stdout as input and output respectively. The getc(stdin) function is equivalent to `getchar()` and the putc(ch, stdout) is equivalent to putchar(ch).

The difference between getc(stdin) and getchar() is that the former reads from a file entered by the input device *i.e.,* keyboard whereas getchar() reads directly from the input device *i.e.,* keyboard.

The functions putc() and putchar() send the character to the standard output device *i.e.,* monitor screen.

Illustration 5. *Write a C program which demonstrates the use of getc() and putc() functions*

```
//use of getc() and putc() functions
#include<stdio.h>
main()
{
    char Ch;
    printf("Enter Character=");
    ch=getc(stdin);
    ch++;
    printf("Next Character will be=");
    putc(ch,stdout);
}
```

Output

```
Enter Character = a
Next Character will be = b
Another output
Enter Character = F
Next Character will be = G
```

❑❑❑

Chapter

Flow of Control, Decision Making and Loops

INTRODUCTION

The normal flow of execution in High Level Languages is in sequential manner, *i.e.,* in the order of their appearance from top to bottom. The statement is executed only once. The programs in which these statements are sequentially executed are called sequential control structure programs. Such programs can be easily modified and underst. But these programs work on limited area and do not fully utilise the capabilities of HLL.

Sometimes a statement is to be altered by the user selectively or repetitively. Various C control structures are used to control the flow of processing.

COMPOUND STATEMENT

Grouping of statements in which individual statement ends with a semi-colon is called compound statement. The grouping of statements is also called **Block.** Compound statement is enclosed between the pair of braces ({}). The opening brace ({) represents the beginning and closing brace (}) represents the end of the block.

The following branching given in the illustration takes place without any decision. It is unconditional branching.

Illustration :

```
{
   printf("Length & Breadth of rectangle");
   scanf("%d%d", &length, &breadth);
   perimeter = 2*(length + breadth);
   printf("Perimeter%d",perimeter);
}
```

CONDITIONAL STATEMENTS

Several times need arises when the program is to be executed depending upon a particular condition. 'If' statement is used for this selective execution. The branching that is based on a particular condition is called condition branching.

'If' Statement

The 'If' statement is used to select one alternative out of the two. The execution of if statement starts with the evaluation of the condition. The 'if' statement, therefore, helps the programmer to test for the condition and is a powerful decision statement.

General Form of 'if' statement :

if expression statement;

Expression can appear in the parentheses of the 'if' statement. If the expression has 0 (zero) value, it is false and if the value is non-zero, this is true. C provides the following constructs for selection control.

— if-construct.

— if-else construct

— if-else-if construct

— if-if-else construct

— switch construct

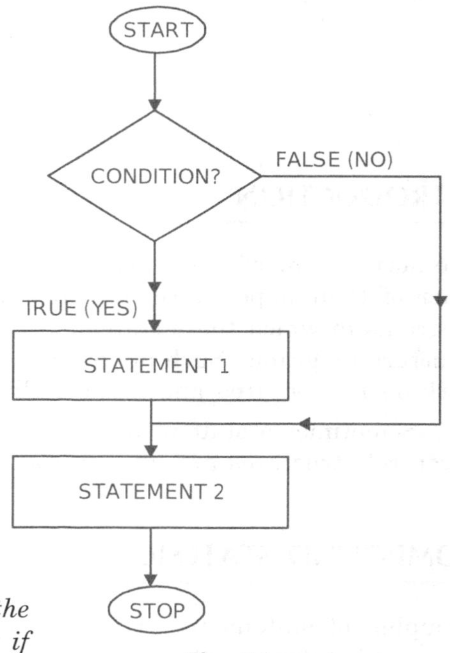

Fig. 6.1

Flow Chart of if-Construct

From the chart it is clear if the condition is true (yes), statement 1 is executed and then statement 2 is executed. If the condition is false (No), statement 1 is not executed and directly statement 2 is executed.

Illustration 1. *Develop a C program to find the greatest number out of the three + ve numbers using if construct*

Solution :

```
//This program finds the greatest of three numbers.
#include<stdio.h>
main()
{
    int a,b,c, greatest;           //a,b,c, are given numbers
    puts("Enter 3 numbers=");      //input a,b,c,
    scanf("%d%d%d",&a,&b,&c);
    greatest=a;                    //greatest is assigned the value
    if(b>greatest)
    greatest =b;
    if(c>greatest)
```

```
greatest=C;
printf("Greatest Number=%d",greatest);
```

Explanation :

In this C program, the greatest identifier is assigned the value of 'a'. The value of 'b' is compared with that of greatest. If b is greatest, the expression is b>greatest.

The statement

greatest = b; is executed

If b<greatest, the statement

greatest = b; is ignored

Now the 'if' statement, compares the value of 'c' with the highest number. If c>greatest, then greatest is assigned the value of C.

A semicolon must not follow the if statement.

if-else Construct

The execution of the 'if-else' statement starts with the evaluation of the condition. The method of testing one condition and then the other works but it is of complex nature. The key word else provides readable code.

```
if(expression)
statement;
else
statement;
```

Flow Chart of if-else Statement

From the chart it is clear if the condition is true, statement 1 is executed followed by statement 3. Statement 2 is not executed. If the condition is false, statement 2 is followed by statement 3. In this case statement 1 is not executed.

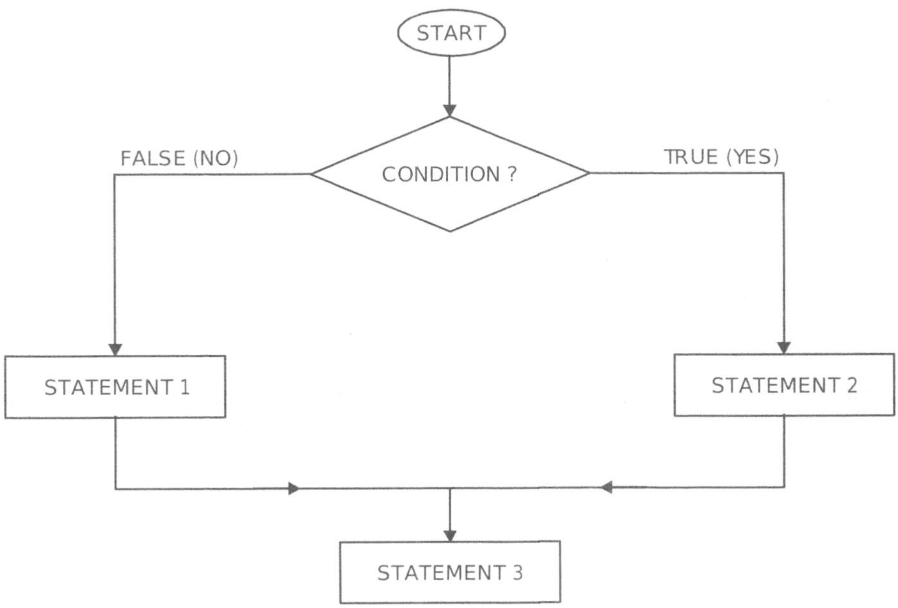

Fig. 6.2

Illustration 2. *Develop a C program to find the value of the following expression, where a,b,c are constants and belong to the data type float.*

$$y = ax^2 + bx + c; \text{ if } x>4$$
$$= -ax^2 + bx - c; \text{ if } x<4$$

Solution :

```
//This program evaluates an expression
#include<stdio.h>
main()
{
    float a,b,c,x,y;
    puts("Enter value of a,b,c,x =");
    scanf("%f%f%f%f",&a,&b,&c,&x);    //value of constant and
                                      //other parameters.
    if(x>=4)
    y=a*x*+x+b*x+c;
    else
    y=a*x*x+b*x-c;
    printf("Value of y=%f",y);
    return0;
}
```

if-else-if Construct

The if-else-if construct can be shown as below :

```
if (condition1)
statement 1
else
if(condition 2)
statement 2
else
if(condition n)
statement n
```

Execution of if-else-if Construct

First of all the condition 1 is tested and if it is true then, statement 1 is executed and all other if-else-if construct ends.

If condition 1 is false, then the statement/is ignored and condition 2 is tested. If it is true then statement 2 is executed and remaining if-else-if construct is terminated and if the conditions 2 is false, statement 2 is ignored and conditions 3 is tested. This process continues in this way.

Illustration 3. *Write a program to calculate the commission of a salesman of books as per following data :*

Sales	*Commission*
More than & Equal to Rs. 100000	25%
Rs. 80000 to Rs. 99999	22.5%
Rs. 60000 to Rs. 79999	20%
Rs. 40000 to Rs. 59999	15%
Less than Rs. 40,000	12.5%

Solution :

```
//This program calculates commission of a salesman on selling books.
#include<stdio.h>
main()
{
    float sales;
    float comm;
    puts("Enter sales=");
    scanf("%f'& sales);
    if(sales>=100000)
    comm=sales*0.25;
    else if(sales>=80000)
    comm=sales *0.225;
    else if(sales>=60000)
    comm=sales*0.2;
    else if(sales>=40000)
    comm=sales*0.15;
    else
    comm=sales*0.125;
    printf("Commission is=%f",comm);
}
```

Output :

```
Enter sales : 74000
The commission is 14800.
```

Illustration 4. *Develop a C program to solve the quadratic equation :*

$$ax^2 + bx + c = 0 \qquad (a \neq 0)$$

Solution : The two values of x can be given by $x = \dfrac{-b \pm \sqrt{b^2 - 4ac}}{2a}$

if $b^2 - 4ac > 0$ roots are real and unequal

if $b^2 - 4ac = 0$ roots are equal and real

if $b^2 - 4ac < 0$ roots are imaginary and unequal

The quantity if $b^2 - 4ac$ is called discriminant and denoted by D.

```
//This program solves a quadratic equation
#include<stdio.h>
#include<math.h>
main()
{
    int a,b,c,;
    float r1, float r2;
    puts("Enter value of a,b,c=");
    scanf("%d,%d,%d" &a,&b,&c);
    if(b*b-4*a*c)>0)
    {
        r1=(-b+sqrt(b*b-4*a*c))/(2*a);
        r2=(-b-sqrt(b*b-4*a*c))/(2*a);
        printf("One root is=%f",r1);
        printf("Second root is=%f",r2);
    }
    else
    if((b*b-4*a*c==0))
    {
        r1=-b/(2*a);
        r2=-b/(2*a);
        printf("root1 is %f",r1);
        printf("root2 is %f",r2);
    }
    else
    if(b*b-4*a*c)<0
    {
        r1=(-b+sqrt(b*b-4*a*c))/(2*a);
        r2=(-b-sqrt(b*b-4*a*c))/(2*a);
        printf("Root1 is imaginary%f",r1);
        printf("Root2 is imaginary%f",r2);
        return 0;
    }
}
```

Run of the Program :

```
Enter the values of a, b, c;
1
4
4
root 1 is -2
root 2 is -2
Another Run of the program
Enter the values of a, b, c;
1
0
-4
```

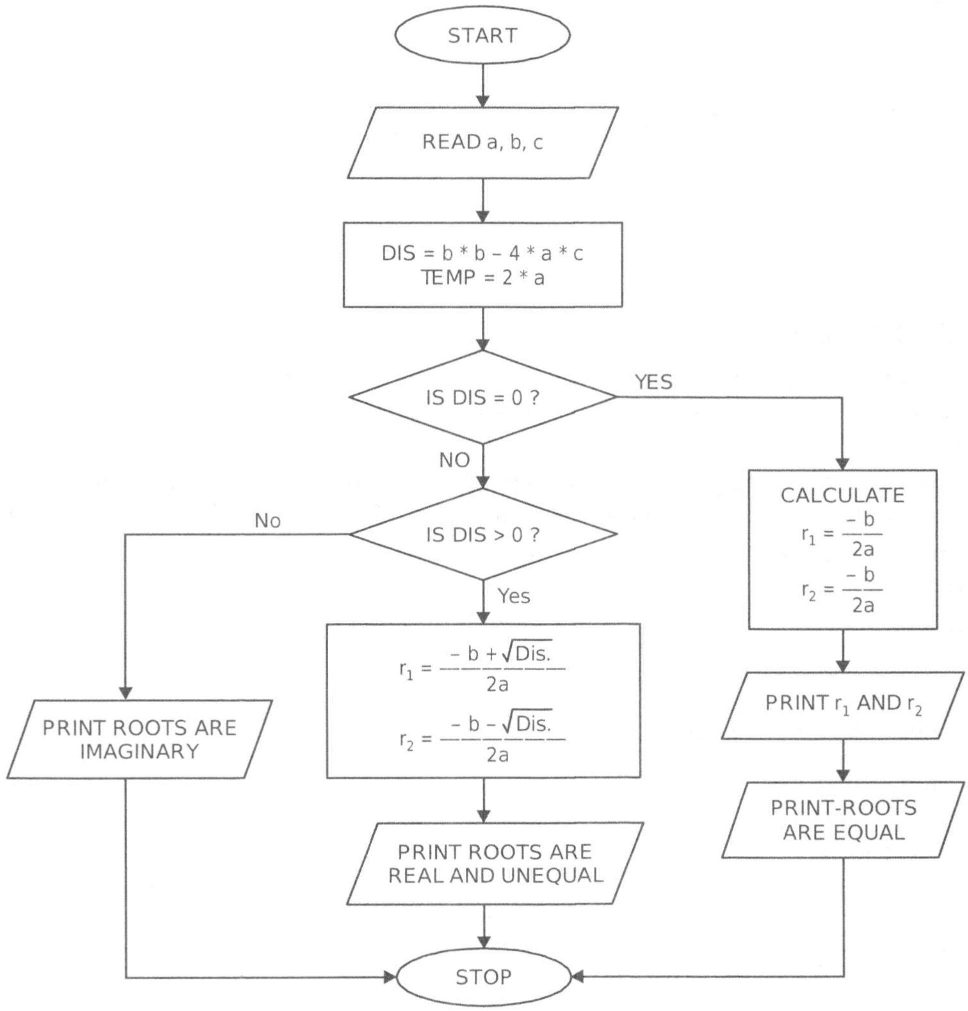

Fig. 6.3

```
One  Root  is  2
Second  Root  is  -2
```

Nested if Statements

If or else can consist another if statement, *i.e.,* the if-else statements can be nested in one another.

Execution of nested if statements has been shown below :

```
if(expression 1)
if(expression 2)
{
    ...................
    ...................
}
```

```
else
if(expression 3)
{
    ...................
    ...................
else
    ...................
    ...................
}
```

The Break Statement

To stop execution and to transfer the control outside the switch body, the break statement is used. This statement is used when you want to skip over a loop instead of exiting the entire program.

The break statement appears in the body of **while, do-while, for** or **switch** statements. The break statement exists the most currently loop. This acts as a jumping instruction.

If a program consists a **while** loop with another while loop, then the **break exits** only the internal loop.

Syntax :

```
break;
```

Consider the following program segments :

```
While(expression)
{
statement 1;
if(amount>15000)
break;
...................
...................
statement 2;
}
statement 3;
```

```
do
{
statement 1;
```

```
if(amount>15000)
break;
   statement 2;
{
while(expression);
statement 3;
```

```
for (int; expression; stop)
{
statement 1;
if(amount)
break;
   statement 2;
}
statement 3;
```

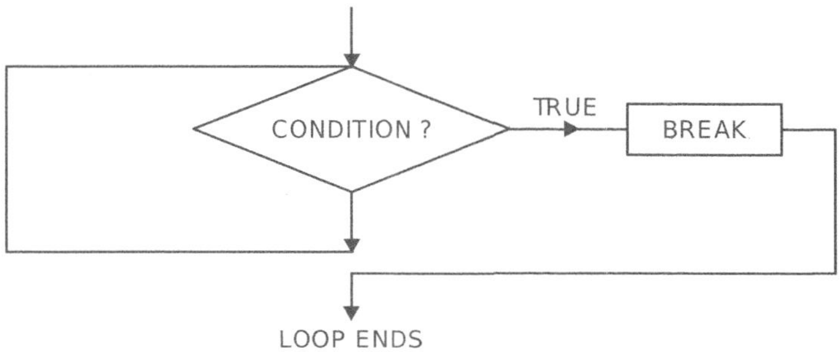

Fig. 6.4 Flow chart for break statement.

Illustration 5. *The following program finds the quotient when one number divides another.*

Solution :

```
//Program to find Quotient.
#include<stdio.h>
main()
int number 1, number 2,i,Q;
for(i=1;i<=20;i++)
{
   puts("Enter first number=")
   scanf("%d",&number1);
   puts("Enter second number=")
   scanf("%d",&number2);
   if(number2==0)
   break;
   else
   Q = number1/number2;
   printf("Quotient is=%",Q)
}
}
```

The above program terminates as soon as the value of number 2 is entered as 0 (zero).

Use of Break Statement in the Nested Loops

Consider the following nested Loops

```
for(int; expression; stop)
{
```

```
    statement 1;
    while(expression)
{

    statement 2;
    if(condition)
    break;
    statement 3;
}


    statement 4;
    if(condition)
    break;
    statement 5;
}


    statement 6;
```

The Continue Statement

The **continue** statement does opposite of the **break** statement. It forces the next **iteration** of the loop. **The break** statement causes termination of the loop and reaches at the bottom at the loop.

In case you use a **continue** statement in the body of **while, do-while,** for loop, the compiler ignores any other statement in the loop that follows the **continue** statement.

General Syntax :

```
continue;
```

```
while(condition)
{

    statement 1;
   if(condition)
       continue;
    statement 2;
}
    statement 3;
              do
{
    statement 1;
   if(condition)
       continue;
    statement 2;
}
while(condition);
   statement; 3;
```

```
for(int; expression; stop)
{
statement 1;
    if(condition)
continue;
statement 2;
}
statement 3;
```

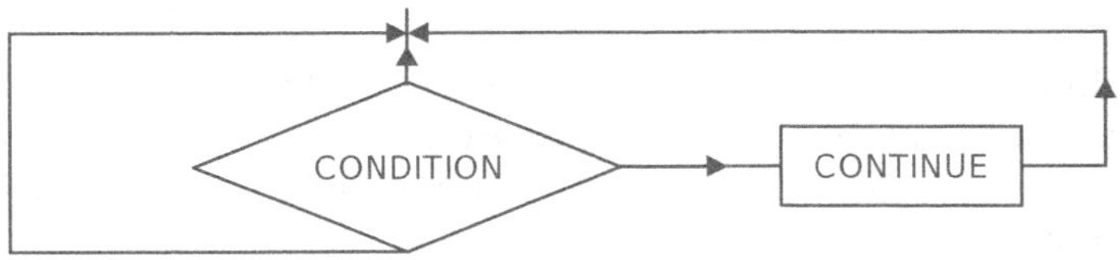

Fig. 6.5

Illustration 6. *The following program finds the Quotient.*

Solution :

```
#include<stdio.h>
main()
int number 1, number 2,i,a;
for(i=1;1<=50;i++)
{
    puts("Enter First number=");
    scanf("%d",number1);
    puts("Enter Second number=");
    scanf("%d",&number2);
    if(number2==0)
    {
       printf("You entered a zero for second number");
       continue;
    }
    else
    Q = number1/number2;
}
}
```

Use of Continue Statement in the Nested Loops

The continue statement can be used in nested loops also.

```
do
{
statement 1;
while(expression)
{
statement 2;
if(condition)
continue;
```

```
statement 3;
{
statement 4;
if(condition)
continue;
statement 5;
{
while (expression);
statement 6;
```

In the above illustration, two loops have been used. These are do loop and while loop. In the **continue** statement in **while** loop, the program execution reaches to the first statement of while loop where the condition is tested. The statements after the **continue** statement in the **while** loop do not execute.

The Switch Statement

Switch is a multi-branch selection construct.

Switch is a powerful construct in C. If one of several courses of action has to be selected, the switch statement can be used.

The syntax of switch statement is given below:

```
switch(expression)
{
case constant 1:
statement sequence 1;
case constant 2:
statement sequence 2;
...............................
...............................
default:
statement sequence;
```

Execution of Switch Statement

The execution of switch statement starts with the evaluation of expression. If the expression evaluates as a constant the execution of switch starts with the statement with constant n. All other statements following this statement execute sequentially. If the value of expression does not reconcile with the constant 1, constant 2....the statement with default is executed.

Flow Chart for Switch Statement

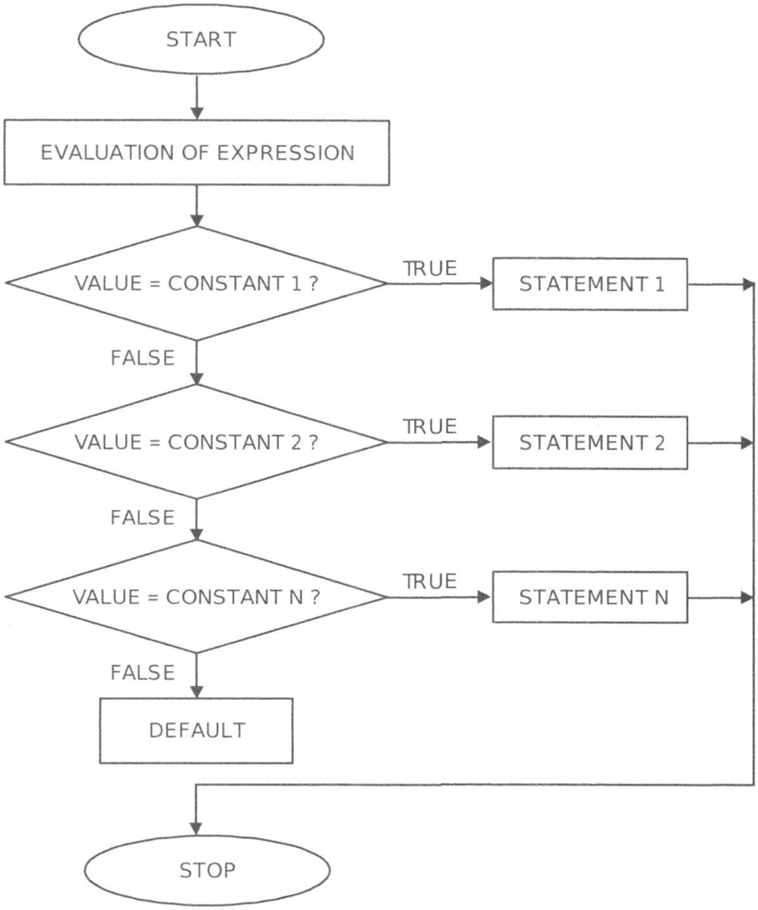

Fig. 6.6

Execution of switch Statement with break Statement

The break statement follows a series of statement and brings the termination of the **Switch Construct.** It then skips over the remaining statements without further execution.

No semicolon is allowed with switch construct. **Case** Statements should be integers or characters. No number with a decimal point should be used with case statement.

EXIT FUNCTION

The `exit()` function terminates the program. It terminates as a break statement.

General Syntax :

```
exit (n);
```

where n is any argument which may be either 0 or 1.

When the exit() function is carried, the program terminates in normal way. If we use exit (1), the program terminates abnormally and with (0) it terminates normally.

Example :

```
main()
{
    ............
    ............
    if(root<=0)
    exit();
    ............
    ............
}
```

Illustration 7. *The following program uses exit( ) function.*

Solution :

```
//use of exit()
#include<stdio.h>
int main()
{
    int number, a;
    puts("Enter number=");
    scanf("%d",&number);
    for(a=2;a<=number,++a)
    if(number %a==0)
    {
        printf("Number is divisible by 7\n");
        exit(0);
    }
    printf("Number is not Divisible by 7");
}
```

Output of the Program :

```
Enter Number = 1414
Number is Divisible by 7
Another Run
Enter Number = 1011
Number is not Divisible by 7
```

In the above program, if the number is divisible by 7 it flashes a message that it is divisible by 7 and exits from the program.

The exit() function does not have return value. Its argument(0) is returned to the system in the above illustration.

LOOP CONSTRUCT

Loop constructs are used for Repetitive Control. Sometimes there is a need of a set of statements to be executed number of times by changing the values of one or more variables each time to obtain a different result. Such execution is called looping. C provides the following loops :

1. while loop
2. do-while loop
3. for loop

The While Loop

The while loop is used for repetitive execution of a program subject to the conditions which may have Zero (False) or Non-Zero (True) value.

General Syntax for the while-loop :

```
while(condition)
{
    body of loop
}
```

while is a key word of C, condition is an expression and the statement can be a simple or compound one.

Flow Chart for the While-Loop

If the condition evaluates to a non-zero (true) execution, the condition is evaluated again and if the condition evaluates to a zero (false) execution, the while-loop terminates.

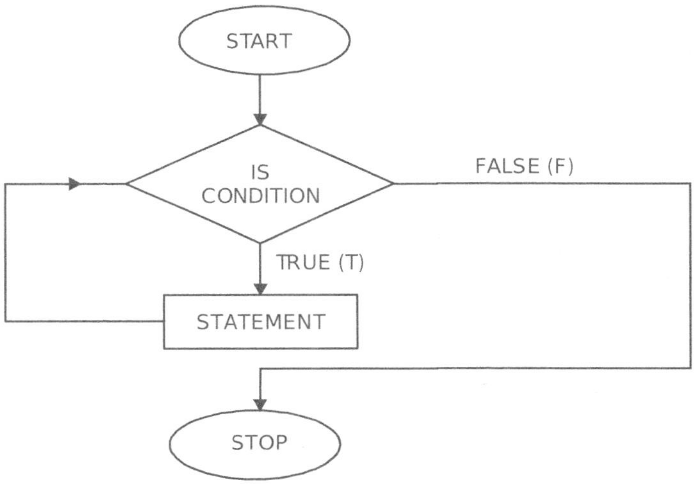

Fig. 6.7

In the above flow chart the loop is repeated again until the condition is true, otherwise terminated

Illustration 8. *Write a C program to compute x^n, where x and n are real integers.*

Solution :

```
//This program computes x^n using the while-loop.
#include<stdio.h>
main()
{
```

```
    float x;
    int n;
    float power;     //read the values of x and n.
    puts("Enter the values=");
    scanf("%f%d",&x,&n);
    power = 1.0;     // set up while loop n times).
    while(n>=1)
    {
       power=power*x;
       n--;
    }
    printf("Power=%f",power);
}
```

Illustration 9. *Write a C program which calculates the average and sum of numbers using while loop.*

Solution :

```
//This program calculates the average and sum of the given numbers using while loop.
#include<stdio.h>
#include<math.h>
main()
{
    int number,i;
    float average, sum;
    puts("How many numbers you want to enter ?");
    scanf("%d", &number);
    sum=0
    i=0;
    while(i<=number-1)
    {
       puts("Enter Number");
       scanf("%f", &x);
       sum=sum+x;
       ++i;
    }
    average =sum/number;
    printf("Sum of the Number is=%f\n", sum);
    printf("Average of the Number is=%f\n", average);
}
```

Run of the Program :

```
How many numbers you want to Enter ? 5
1
2
3
4
5
Sum of the Numbers is = 15
Average of the Numbers is = 3
```

The Do-While Loop

The do-while loop is another repetitive control structure. It is also called exit-controlled loop executing the body of the loop. In while-loop the condition is tested before execution whereas in a do-while loop the condition is tested after execution.

General Syntax :

```
do
{
statement;
}
while (condition);
```

Condition may be a single or compound statement. The condition may have 0 or non-Zero.

The difference between while and do while loop is that in while loop if condition is false, the loop will not be executed even once but in case if do while loop even if the condition is false, the loop will be executed.

do-while	*while*
1. The loop executes the statement at least once, inspite the condition is false.	1. The loop cannot be executed even once it the condition is false.
2. The condition is tested after execution of body of loop.	2. The condition is tested before execution of body of loop.
3. If the condition is false, the computer keeps executing the loop.	3. The loop terminates if the condition becomes false.
4. Semicolon (;) is placed after do while statement.	4. No semicolon is placed after while condition.

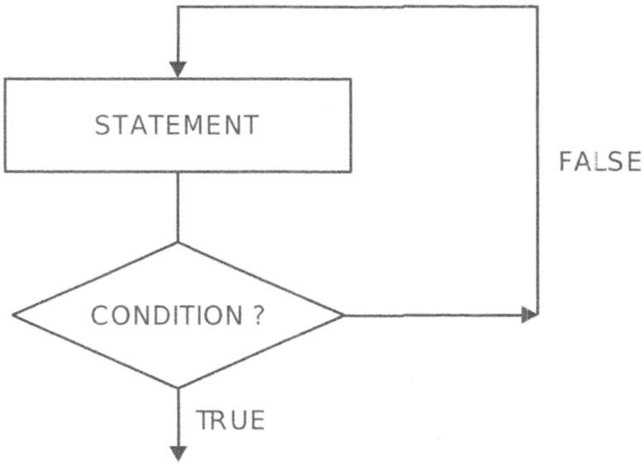

Fig. 6.8

Illustration 10. *Develop a C program which counts the number of bounces a rubber ball makes before it stops bouncing.*

It is assumed that the ball reaches to 0.9 times of its previous bounce (height) The ball is considered to be at rest if the height of the bounce is less than 0.5 cm above the ground.

Given the initial height is 3 metres.

Solution :

```
//This program counts the number of bounces.
#include<stdio.h>
main()
{
   int count;
   float height;
   count=0;                      //initialise count
   puts("Enter the height");
   scanf("%f", height);          //read height
   //set up the do-while loop
   //do loop starts
   do
   {
      height=height*0.9;
      count++;
   }
   while(height>0.5);            //while condition
   printf("The number of bounces is %d", count);
}
```

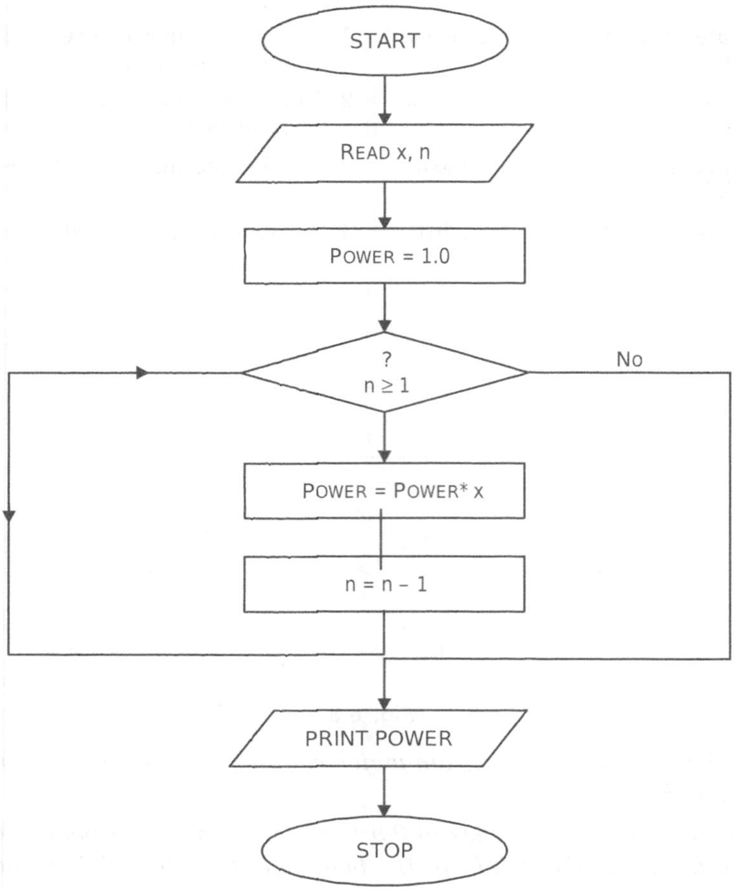

Fig. 6.9

Illustration 11. *Write a program in C which calculates the average and sum of the given number using do-while loop.*

Solution :

```
//This program calculates the average and sum of the given numbers using do-
while loop.
#include<stdio.h>
#include<math.h>
main()
{
   int number,i;
   float average;
   float sum;
   float x;
   puts("How many numbers you want to enter ?");
   scanf("%d", &number);
   sum=0;
   i=0;
   do
   {
      puts("Enter Number");
      scanf("%f", &x);
      sum=sum + x;
      i++;
   }
   while (i<=number-1);
   average=sum/number;
   printf("Sum of These Numbers is= "%f\n",sum);
   printf("Average of the Numbers is= "%f\n",average);
}
```

Run of the Program :

```
How many numbers you want to enter ? 5
1
2
3
4
5
Sum of These Numbers is = 15
Average of the Numbers is = 3
```

Illustration 12. *Determine the Product of first n natural number.*

Solution :

```
//This program determines the product of first n natural number
#include<stdio.h>
main()
```

```
{
    int n, product;
    puts("Enter Value of n=");
    scanf("%d",&n);
    for(int i=0; product=0; i=n;i ++)
    product=product+i;
    printf("The product of first n natural numbers" =%d, product);
    return 0;
}
```

Illustration 13. *What will be the output of the following program ?*

```
#include<stdio.h>
main()
{
    int a;
    for(a=0;a<=20;++a)
    {
        printf("%d",a);
    }
}
```

Solution : Output of the program

0 1 2 3 4 5 6 7 8 9 10 11 12 13 14 15 16 17 18 19 20

The For-Loop

The for statement is the most commonly used iterative statement in Java.

The for-loop is also used for repetitive execution of C program but for a fixed number of times. The program knows well in advance how many times the loop is to be executed.

In for loop, the imitialisation test expression and update expression are placed at one place.

General Syntax :

```
for(initial expression; test expression;
        update expression)
{
    statement
}
```

Execution of a For-Loop

1. First of all the initial expression is evaluated.
2. In next step, the test-expression is evaluated.
   If the value is non-zero, the loop is executed otherwise
   If the value is zero, the loop is terminated without any future execution.
3. After the execution of for-loop, the update expression is evaluated.
   Flow Chart for Execution of For-Loop.

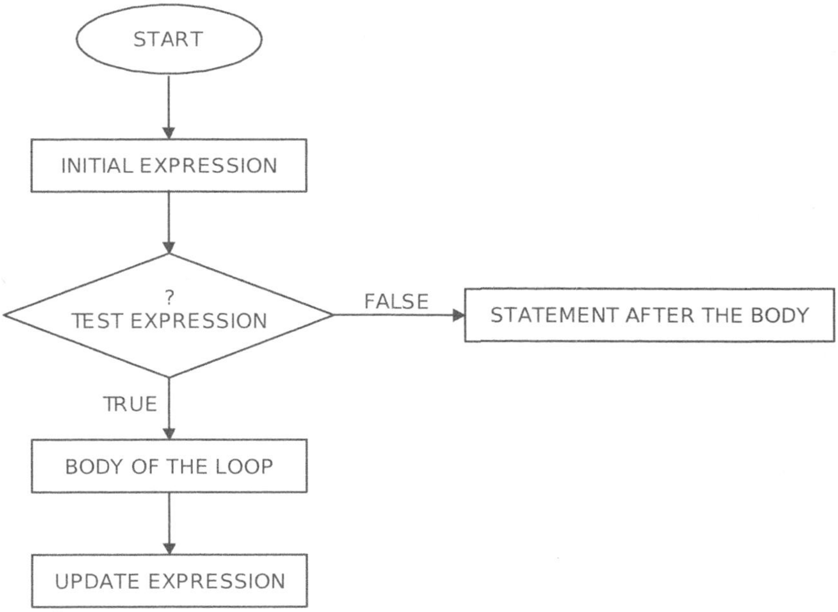

Fig. 6.10

Points to Note :

1. The loop begins with the 'for' statement with parentheses.
2. Initial, test and update expressions all are placed within parentheses in a specific order. For example :

   for(a=0; a<= 10; a++)

3. The statements to the executed repeatedly are placed in a sequence within the body of the loop.

Illustration 14. *Write a program to find the square of first 20 numbers using* ***for*** *loop.*

Solution :

```
//This program demonstrates the use of for loop.
#include<stdio.h>
main()
{
   int a;
   for(a=0;a<=20;++a)
   printf("%d",a*a);
}
```

Output of the program :

```
0 1 4 9 16 25 36 49 64 81 100 121 144 169 196 225 256 289 324 361 400
```

Illustration 15.

Solution :

```
//This program finds even number up to 100.
#include<stdio.h>
main()
{
```

```
    int number;
    for(number=2;number<=100;number=number+2;){
    printf("%d",number);
}
}
```

ADDITIONAL PROGRAMS

1. *Write a C program to calculate the sum and average of the given numbers. (Use do-while loop).*

Solution :

```
//This program calculates the sum and average of the given numbers
#include<stdio.h>
#include<math.h>
void main(void)
{
    int i,N;
    float average, x, sum;
    puts("Enter the Count of the Numbers");
    scanf("%d",N);
    i=0;
    sum=0;
    do
    {
       puts("Enter a Number");
       scanf("%f",&x);
       sum=sum+x;
       i++;
    }
    while(i<=N-1);
    average=sum/N;
    printf("The sum of given Numbers is %f, sum);
    printf("Average is %f", average);
}
```

2. *Write a C program which calculate the sum of even numbers. (Use do-while loop).*

Solution :

```
//This program calculates the sum of given even numbers using do-while loop.
#include<stdio.h>
#include<math.h>
void main(void)
{
    int MAX,NUMBER,SUM;
    NUMBER=2;
    puts("Enter a Number:");
    scanf("%d",&MAX);
```

```
    SUM=0;
    do
    {
       SUM=SUM+NUMBER;
       NUMBER=NUMBER+2;
    }
    while(NUMBER<=MAX);
    printf("\2+4+6+8+....%d\n",MAX);
    printf("SUM%d\n",SUM);
}
```

The output of the above program will be :

```
Enter a Number : 12
2 + 4 + 6 + 8 +..... 12
SUM = 42
```

3. *Write a C program to demonstrate the use of compound if statement*

Solution :

```
//This program demonstrates the use of compound if statement
#include<stdio.h>
void main(void)
{
    int AGE;
    puts("Enter age of the Child:");
    scanf("%d",&AGE);
    if(AGE<0)
    {
       printf("\It's invalid age %d\n");
       printf("\My Dear Friend %d\n");
       printf("\Age cannot be Negative%d\n");
       return0;
    }
    if (AGE<18)
    printf("You are under age, my dear");
```

The output of the program will be :

```
Enter age of the Child : – 6
It's invalid age
My Dear Friend
Age cannot be Negative
```

4. *Write a C program which prints the list of numbers between 1 to 500 which are exactly divisible by 20.*

Solution :

```
//This program finds the list of numbers between 1 to 500 exactly divisible by 20.
#include<stdio.h>
main()
{
    int n=0;
    printf("The numbers are =%d\n");
    while(n<=500)
    {
       if(n%20!=0)
       continue;
       else
       printf(n);
    }
}
```

5. *Write a C program to check whatever a number is odd, even or prime.*

Solution :

```
//This program verifies whether a number is odd, even or prime
//using if-else-if loop.
#include<stdio.h>
main()
{
    int i, number;
    char chr;
    do
    {
       puts("Enter Number:");
       scanf("%d",&number);
       if(number%2==0)
       printf("The number is Even");
       else
       printf("odd");
       if(number==1)
       printf("The number is also Prime");
       else
       {
          for(i=2;i<=number/2;++i)
          if(number%i==0)
          printf("The number is Not Prime");
          goto lb;
       }
       printf("The number is also Prime");
    }
    ib;
```

```
    puts("Want to continue(Yes/No)"?);
    scanf("%c",chr);
    }
    while (chr=='Y'||chr=='y');
    return 0;
}
```

Ouput of the Program :

```
Enter Number : 7
Odd
The number is also Prime
Want to continue (Yes/No)?Y
Enter Number : 28
The number is Even
The number is Not Prime
Want to Continue (Yes/No)?
```

6. *Write a C program which finds the divisors of the given number.*

Solution :

```
//This program finds the divisors of the given number.
#include<stdio.h>
main()
{
    int number, divisor;
    puts("Enter the number")
    scanf("%d",&number);
    clrscr();
    for(divisor=1;divisor<=number/2;++divisor)
    {
       if(number%divisor==0)
       printf("One of the divisors of this number is %d\n",divisior);
    }
    return 0;
}
```

7. *Write a C Program which checks whether a year is a leap year or not.*

Solution :

```
//This program checks whenever a year is a leap year or not using if-else loop.
#include<stdio.h>
main()
{
    int year;
    puts("Enter the year");
    scanf("%d",&year);
    if(year%4==0&&year%100!=0||year%400==0)
    printf("It is a leap year");
```

```
    else
    printf("It is not a leap year")
}
```

Output of the Program :

```
Enter the year : 1996
It is a leap year
Another run of the Program :
Enter the year : 1999
It is not a leap year.
```

8. *Write a program to find the sum of series :*

S = 1 + (1 + 2) + (1 + 2 + 3) + (1 + 2 + 3 + 4) +..............upto n terms.

Solution :

```
//This program finds the sum of series.
#include<stdio.h>
main()
{
    int sum = 0,i,n,t=0;
    puts("Enter the value of n");
    scanf("%d",&n);
    for(i=1; i<=n;i++)
    {
        t+=i;
        sum+=t;
        printf("The Sum of the Series is=%d",sum);
    }
```

Output of the Program :

```
Enter the value of n : 20
The Sum of the Series is = 1540.
```

9. *Write a program which sums the cube of digits of a given number. [Example 123 = $1^3 + 2^3 + 3^3$]*

Solution :

```
#include<stdio.h>
#include<conio.h>
main()
{
    int a,b, sum, d;
    int number;
    puts("Enter the number");
    scanf("%d",&number);
    for(a=1;a<=number;a++)
    {
```

```
        sum = 0;
        b = a;
        while(b!=0)
        {
            d=b%10;
            sum=sum+d*d*d;
            b = b/10;
        }
        if(sum==a)
        printf("sum of cubes of digits of the number=%d\n,a);
    }
    getch();
    }
    scanf("%d",&n");
    y = sqrt (n);
    x = y*Y;
    if(x==n)
    printf("The number is perfect");
    else
    printf("The number is perfect:");
    return 0;
}
}
```

❑❑❑

Chapter

Functions in C

INTRODUCTION

A programmer can write lengthy programs but length of the programs is not of significance if the program cannot be understood by others. The capability of the programmer is observed in terms of readable programs created with clear functions and with the length.

It is better for the programmer himself to write programs with smaller functions. language consists of many functions and programmer can use simple or complex functions. It is always better to break a large program into smaller units.

WHAT IS A FUNCTION?

A function is a sub-program which can act on data and produce a result. In C, the function should be defined before its usage in the program.

General Syntax :

```
type function-name(formal-argument list)
```

Every C program has at least one main function that is main (). When the program stars, the function main () is automatically called and this can call other function/functions it cannot be called by any other function.

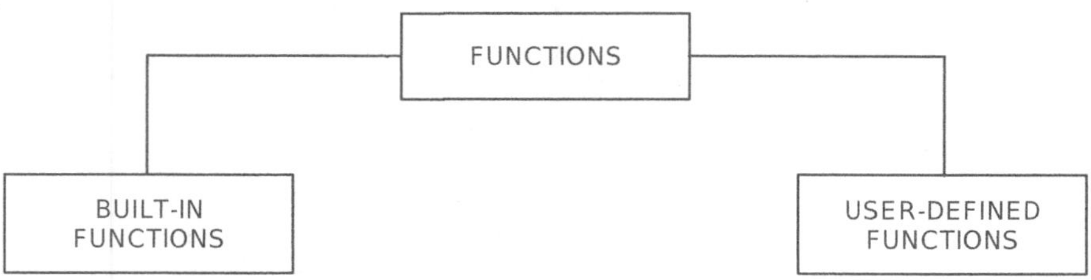

Fig. 7.1

Built-in functions are called library functions and they are the part of compiler leakage. User-defined functions are used according to the requirement of the program is created by the programmer himself.

Sometimes a function has to be used in programs, then it is advisable to place this function in a separate header file. When the same function is to be used, the header file is included in the program.

C provides standard header files in which contain variety of function. These standard functions are used in the program by writing the name of the functions with appropriate argument (parameter list) which is written within parentheses.

Declaring and Defining a Function

First of all declare the function in the program and then define it.

This declaration is called Function Prototype and this tells the compiler about name, return type parameters of the function. The function definition tells the compiler how a function works in the program. Many built-in functions have their own prototypes. The files having these prototypes are included in the program by using—

#include

The definition of a function consists of the function header. The statements enclosed within { and } is called the body of the function.

General Syntax:

```
Type function-name(formal argument list)
{ Opening Brace                       }
            Statements                } Body of the
            return expression;        } function.
} closing Brace
```

Function Prototypes

All functions should be declared before their use in a program. The prototype tells the computer about characteristics of the function being used in the program. Many built-in functions have their function prototypes already written. The files having these prototypes should be included in the program by using #include directive. In user-defined functions, prototype is included in the source code.

General form :

```
<type><name>(arguments);
```

The function prototype is a statement which ends with a semicolon.

There are 3 main components in function prototype :

1. Function Name
2. Function Type
3. Function Arguments.

Function Name

It is user defined any legal identifier followed by parentheses without any space.

Function Type

The function 'type' is the type of value to be returned. Every function has a return type. If a function does not return a value, its return type will be void.

Function Arguments

Function arguments is a list of parameters. The arguments are placed in the parentheses. All function arguments need not be of same type. A function can have integer character as its arguments. Any valid C expression may be a function argument that includes constants, logical expression and other functions that return a value. If the function does not use any argument, the word void is used within the parentheses. Void is a signal to the compiler that no value is to be returned.

The function that does not return a value and that does not require any parameter is declared as follows :

```
void function-name (parameter list);     //does not return a value
type; function name(void);               //does not require parameter
```

Examples of Function Prototypes

```
void volume();
float volume(int l, float b, float h);
int volume(int a, int b, int c);
```

Accessing a Function

An accessing function can be called or invoked in/form the main program by using function name, followed by the parameters enclosed in parentheses separated by commas. It should be noted that in the function definition in the beginning, the semicolon is not used at the end. If semicolon is absent, it means that you are defining a function and not calling it. Therefore, when a function is called, it is necessary to keep semicolon at the end. A function call statement may be written as follows :

volume( );

This statement will transfer the control to function volume(). By using the following statement we can call the function clear

clear( );

When a call statement is encountered, the control is transferred to the function.

Illustration 1. *Write a C program which illustrates function accessing and prototyping.*

Solution :

```
//This program illustrates function accessing and prototyping.
#include<math.h>
#include<iomanip.h>
main()
{
   float square (float); //function prototype
```

```
    float a,b;
    puts("Enter the Number");
    scanf("%f",&a);
    b=square(a);
    printf("The Square of the Number is=%f",b);
    return0;
}
float square (float c)
{
    return c*c;
}
```

Run of the Program :

```
Enter the Number : 5
The Square of the Number is = 25
→(Transfer of Control)
```

When the function call statement is given then the control automatically transfers to functions body and statements are executed.

Writing Your Own Functions

A function has the following layout:

```
return-type function-name ( argument-list-if-necessary )
{
    ...local-declarations...
    ...statements...
    return return-value;
}
```

If `return-type` is omitted, C defaults to `int`. The `return-value` must be of the declared type.

A function may simply perform a task without returning any value, in which case it has the following layout :

```
void function-name ( argument-list-if-necessary )
{
    ...local-declarations...
    ...statements...
}
```

As an example of function calls, consider the following code :

```
#include<stdio.h>
#include<string.h>
                        // prototyping of functions
```

```
void main()
{
   int n;
   char string[25];
                        // strcpy (a,b) copies string b into a
                        // defined via the stdio.h header
   strcpy(string, "Hello World");
                        // call own function
   n = n_char(string);
   printf("Length of string = %d\n",n);
}

                        // definition of local function n_char
int n_char (string[])
{
                        // local variable in this function
   int n;
                        // strlen (a) returns the length of
                        // string a
                        // defined via the string.h header
   n=strlen(string);
   if(n>25)
      printf("String is longer than 25 characters\n");

                        // return the value of integer n
   return n;
}
```

Arguments are always passed *by value* in C function calls. This means that local "copies" of the values of the arguments are passed to the routines. Any change made to the arguments internally in the function are made only to the local copies of the arguments. In order to change (or define) an argument in the argument list, this argument must be passed as an address, thereby forcing C to change the "real" argument in the calling routine.

As an example, consider exchanging two numbers between variables. First let's illustrate what happen if the variables are passed by value :

```
#include<stdio.h>

void exchange(int a, int b);

void main()
{                       // WRONG CODE
   int a, b;

   a=5;
   b=7;
```

```
    printf("From main: a=%d, b=%d\n", a, b);

    exchange(a,b);
    printf("Back in main:");
    printf("a=%d, b=%d\n", a, b);
}

void exchange(int a, int b)
{
    int temp;

    temp = a;
    a=b;
    b=temp;
    printf("From function exchange:");
    printf("a=%d, b=%d\n", a, b);
}
```

Run this code and observe that a and b are NOT exchanged. Only the copies of the arguments are exchanged. The RIGHT way to do this is of course to use pointers :

```
#include<stdio.h>

void exchange(int *a, int *b);

void main()
{                       //RIGHT CODE
    int a, b;

    a=5;
    b=7;
    printf("From main: a=%d, b=%d\n", a, b);

    exchange(&a,&b);
    printf("Back in main:");
    printf("a=%d, b=%d\n", a, b);
}

void exchange(int *a, int *b)
{
    int temp;

    temp = *a;
    *a = *b;
    *b = temp;
    printf("From function exchange:");
    printf("a=%d, b=%d\n", *a, *b);
}
```

The rule of thumb here is that

- Use regular variables if the function does not change the values of those arguments.
- Use pointers if the function changes the values of those arguments.

Passing Arguments to Function

In a C program we can call a function or a number of functions from another function. The various functions can be called from main() function. If the communication between these functions (calling function and called function), is to be made in such a way that there should be not error then the mechanism of passing variables from one function to the other should be correct one.

Recursion

A function has capability to call itself in a process. This process is called recursion. Recursion may be direct or indirect. When a function calls itself, it is direct recursion and if it calls another function, which then calls first function then it is indirect recursion. Sometimes a function uses not parameters (arguments) but it is capable of returning a value. For example, when we dial Telephone No. 100, we do not speak anything but from other side a reply is received "Police Control Room". No message is given but information is received. The function which does not use arguments can return a value without giving it any information. It returns the value of first character typed on input medium, *i.e.,* keyboard.

The function that have parameters can be accessed in the following ways :

1. Call by Value
2. Call by Reference.

Consider the following example :

```
#include<stdio.h>
int main()
{
    int square(int);
    int volume, side=4;
    .........
    .........
    volume=square(side);  ──┐
    .........               │
    .........               │
    puts("Volume");         │   Invoking of function
    return0;                │
}                        ←──┘
int square(ints) ──┐
return s*s;        │
}                  ↓
            The function square() uses the value of side(i.e., 4) here.
                (call by value)
```

Illustration 2. *Write a program for finding the factorial of a given number by recursion.*

Solution :

```
/* program to find factorial by recursion*/
#include<stdio.h>
long int fact(int);
main()
{
    int n;
    printf("Enter the Number");
    scanf("%d",&n);
    printf("\nFactorial of %d is %1d\n",n, fact (n));
}
long int fact(int n)
{
    if (n==0)
    return(1);
    else
    return(n*fact(n-1));
}
```

One run of the program is given below :

```
Enter the Number : 5
Factorial of 5 is 120
```

Illustration 3. *The following function sums up the squares of the values of variables.*

Solution :

```
#include<stdio.h>
void square(int a, int b, int c);
main()
{
    int x,y,z;
    puts("Enter Values for x,y,z");
    scanf("%d%d%d",&x,&y,&z);
    square(x,y,z);
    printf("x=%d\n",x);
    printf("y=%d\n",y);
    printf("z=%d\n",z);
}
void square(int x, int y, int z)
{
    x = x*x;
    y = y*y;
    z = z*z;
    printf("square of x + square of y + square of z=%d\n",x+y+z);
    return;
}
```

Output of the program :

```
Enter Values for x, y, z
3 4 5
x = 3
y = 4
z = 5
square of x + square of y + square of z = 50
```

Illustration 4 :

```
//Program to illustrate the use of call by reference.
#include<stdio.h>
#include<conio.h>
#include<math.h>
main()
{
    void swap(int *x, int *y);     //Function prototype to accept two reference
                                   //variables
    int x,y;
    x=5,y=10;
    puts("The values before swapping are");
    printf("x=%d",x);
    printf("y=%d",y);
    swap(&a,&b);
    puts("The values after swapping are");
    printf("x=%d\n",x);
    printf("y=%d\n",y);
}
void swap(int &a, int &b)
{
    int change;
    change=*x;
    *x = *y;
    *b=change;
}
```

Run of the Program :

```
The values before swapping are x = 5 y = 10
The values after swapping are x = 10
                                 y = 5.
```

Default Arguments

A C function prototype that can declare one or more arguments of the function have default values. The default values are specified at the time of function declaration. When a call to the function omits the corresponding parameter argument, the compiler inserts the default values.

A function which does not have explicit return value by default returns a value of type int. The function that does not return a value should declare a return type of void. In C program, the functions which does not indicate a return type returns an integer value.

Example :

float interest(float principal int time, float rate=0.6);

comp_int=(6000,3); //third argument missing

The value 6000 passes to the argument principal and value 3 passes to the argument time since the third argument for rate is missing, we can use default value 0.6 as rate.

Now if the initialization is done as :

comp_int=int(6000, 3,0.6); //no argument is missing

here argument principal gets value 6000

Argument time gets value 3

and argument rate gets value 0.6

Note : *It is to be noted until and unless the argument/s on right side has/have default, the argument on immediate left cannot have default value.*

A function which does not have explicit return value by default returns a value of type int. The function which does not return A value should declare a return types of void. In C program, the function which does not indicate a return type returns an integer value.

Study the following declarations :

(*i*) float interest (float principal=6000, int time=3, float rate=0.6);

(*ii*) float interest (float principal=6000, int time=3, float rate);

(*iii*) float interest (float principal, int time=3, float rate=0.6);

(*iv*) float interest (float principal=6000, int time, float rate=0.6);

(*v*) float interest (float principal, int time, float rate=0.6);

— First declaration is valid.

— Second declaration is invalid because the right argument has no default but left arguments have default.

— Third declaration is valid because right arguments have defaults.

— Fourth declaration is invalid because left arguments Principal has default value but the right argument 'time' does not have.

— Fifth declaration is valid because only the right most argument has default value.

Constant Argument

Sometimes when arguments are not to be modified in the function, these are declared as constant arguments. If constant values are assigned to the function, then the function is not able to modify the values. Constant arguments are useful when the function is called by reference.

Call by Value

The function having arguments can be accessed in two ways. One is call by value and the other is call by reference. It is better to first know what is actual and formal parameter.

Actual parameter means the parameter which happens to be present in a function call statement and formal parameter means the parameter which happens to be in function definition. A call by value method copies the value of actual parameter into formal parameter.

Illustration 5. *Consider the following program. It initializes an integer number to 10 and uses a function to add 1 to it.*

Solution :

```
#include<stdio.h>
int add(int);
main()
{
    int n = 10;
    printf("Value of n before Function Call=%d\n", n);
    add(n);
    printf("Value of n after Function Call=%d\n", n);
}
add(int n)
{
    n=n+1;
    printf("Value of n in Function is %d\n", n);
    return(n);
}
```

Run of the Program :

```
Value of n before Function Call = 10
Value of n after Function Call = 11
Value of n in Function is 10
```

Illustration 6 :

```
//The following program finds fibonacci numbers.
#include<stdio.h>
long fib(long n);
main()
{
    long n;
    puts("Enter Positive Integer");
    scanf("%ld",&n);
    printf("%ld\n", fib(n));
}
long fib(long n)
{
    long n1, n2, m=0, s1=0, s2=0, sum=0;
    n1=n2=1;
    m=3;
    while(m<=n)
    {
      sum = n1+n2;
```

```
        s2 = sum;
        if(s2>n)return s1;
        n1 = n2;
        n2 = sum;
        s1 = sum;
        m++;
    }
}
```

Illustration 7 :

```
//To calculate GCD of numbers */
#include<stdio.h>
long gcd();
main()
{
    long num[20], hcf;
    int a,b;
    puts("How many numbers?");
    scanf("%d",&b);
    puts("Enter numbers");
    for(a=0;a<b;++a)
    scanf("%ld",&num[a]);
    hcf = num[0];
    for(a=1;a<b;++a)
    hcf=gcd(gcd,num[m]);
    printf("HCF=%ld\n",hcf);
}
long gcd(long n1, long n2)
{
    int j,r;
    {
        j=n1/n2;
        r=n1-n2*j;
        if(r==0)
    break;
        n1=n2;
        n2=r;
    }
    return(n2);
}
```

Output of the program :

```
How many numbers?
3
Enter numbers
6 27 42
HCF = 3
```

Program

Write a program in C by using function to find the roots of a quadratic equation

$$ax + bx + c = 0$$

```
#include<studio.h>
float roots(float ,float ,float);     //function prototype
main()
{
    float a,b,c;
    printf("Enter value of a,b,c");
    scanf("%f%f%f",&a,&b,&c);
    roots(a,b,c);
}
float roots(float a,float b,float c)
{
    float r1,r2,d;
    d=b*b-4*a*c;
    if(d>0)
    {
       printf("Roots are not equal\n");
       r1=(-b+sqrt(d))/2*a;
       r2=(-b-sqrt(d))/2*a;
       printf("Root1=%2f\n",r1);
       printf("Root2=%2f\n",r2);
    }
    else if(d==0)
    {
       r1=-b/2*a;
       r2=r1;
       printf("Root1 = %2f\n",r1);
       printf("Root2 = %2f\n",r2);
    }
    else
    printf("Roots are imaginary");
    return;
}
```

Call by Reference

Call by reference is frequently used for passing arguments or parameters by reference. Instead of passing a value to the function being called, reference is passed to the original variable. The same variable value can be called by any of the two names, *i.e.,* original variables name and the reference name.

Suppose computer lab of your college is in Room No. 5. Somebody visits your college and enquires about computer teacher. You can either tell him by giving the original name. *i.e.,* Computer Room or Room No. 5. They refer to same place. Similarly original variable's name and reference refer to same memory location.

This method is very useful in C programs where the original variables are to be changed with others by using a function. When a function receives parameter by reference the references are attached to the actual arguments provided by the function (calling function).

Illustration 8. *Write a C program which illustrates passing of arguments by reference.*

Solution :

```
//This program illustrates passing of argument by reference.
#include<stdio.h>
void swap(int &a, int &b)
{
    int x;
    x=a;
    a=b;
    b=x;
}
main()
{
    int i,j;
    i=5;
    j=10;
    puts("Values before Swapping=");
    scanf("%d",&i);
    scanf("%d",&j);
    swap(i,j);
    puts("Values After Swapping=");
    scanf("%d",&i);
    scanf("%d",&j);
}
```

In this illustration `j` is the reference and `i` is the original value.

Some Points to be Noted

1. When a function returns a value in the form of integer (a value of type int) it is called integer function and if it returns the value other than type int (a value of type float), it is called non-integer function.
2. Only variables can be passed in reference and not the constants or expressions.

RETURN BY REFERENCE

A function is capable of returning a reference. Consider the following function

```
int &max(int&a,int&b)
{
    if(a>b)
    return a;
    else
    return b;
}
```

Return type of max() is int&. The function returns reference to a or b. If we call a function such as max (x, y), it will give a reference either to x or y on their values

max(x, y) = –5

It assigns–5 to x (if x>y) otherwise–5 to y (y>x)

CALLING FUNCTIONS WITH ARRAYS

When an array is used as argument to a function, the address of the array is passed and not the whole copy of the array. When a function is called with array name, a pointer to the first element in the array is passed into the function.

Computer stores an array into its memory. An array is referred to by its address. Passing an array name to a function does not make a fresh copy of the array.

While calling function with arrays the following points should be kept in mind.

1. The value of elements in the array.
2. The names of elements in the array.
3. The address of the array in memory.
4. The list of address.

The size of array should also be kept in mind. Arrays are one-dimensional, two-dimensional or multi-dimensional. The size of multi-dimensional array should be specified while there is no need for specification in case of simple-dimensional array. The size of array can be very large, but in C programming we have only one copy of an array and this is why instead of passing values, only the address of the array is passed.

Illustration 9. *Write a C program that finds the sum of values in the array elements.*

Solution :

```
//This program obtains the sum of values in array elements.
#include<stdio.h>
int main()
int sum_arr(int array[],int n)
{
    int total =0;
    for(int i=0;i<n;i++);
    total=total+arr[i];
    return total;
}
int main(void)
{
    int sum[size]={1,8,27,64,125,216,343,512};    //initialization
    int sum1 =sum_arr(sum, size);
    printf("Sum of the elements in the array:", sum1);
    return 0;
}
```

In the above program sum_arr function has been used to find the sum of values. Array has been initialized and uses sum_arr function to calculate the sum.

Let us have a look how to pass a value and array address to a function.

Taking a general function of finding the sum of values of the elements in the array :

1 ⟶ sum_arr() — It is a function

2 ⟶ int — It is type of array

3 ⟶ arr — It tells the array address

4 ⟶ arr[ ] — Indicates pointer

5 ⟶ int n — Indicates the number of elements in the array to be processed.

GLOBAL AND LOCAL VARIABLES

A variable which is defined outside a function is called **Global Variable.** A global variable is available to all the functions which are defined in the file. Global variables, through out the execution, hold their values. Global variables can be accessed from within any function if it is declared properly otherwise it cannot be accessed. The use of global variables however results in complexity but they produce faster code.

In contrast to global variables, local variables are defined within a function. A local variable can have the same name as the global variable has. In such a situation when the name of local variable is same as of global variable, the function hides the global variable.

STORAGE CLASS SPECIFIERS

A storage class specifiers of variables specifies the compiler how it should be stored. C handles the variable according to its storage class.

Types of Storage Class Specifiers

1. Auto
2. Static
3. Register
4. Extern

Auto

This refers to automatic variable. A local variable can be defined by Auto specifier. This specifier is not frequently used. By default, variable defined within a function is auto or automatic. An auto variable is only recognized within the function where and in which it is defined. Let us have a look on the following program segment :

```
void some()
{
    int max_val;
    auto int min_val;
}
```

The function contains two variables max_val and min_val. These variables are created when the function is called. These variables disappear when the function is finished and control is returned to calling function. Variable max_val is local and by default it is automatic whereas the variable min_val has been made automatic explicitly by using key word auto. Both the variables are equivalent in terms of scope and their effect is exactly same. There the key word auto creates only confusion and has no use.

Lifetime

Lifetime is an important characteristic of automatic variable. The name auto in a program is used since the variables are automatically created when a function is called and when the function is returned, the variables are destroyed. The time period between creation of variables and their destruction is called **lifetime.** The lifetime of auto variable is the time when the function, in which it has been defined, is executing.

The limiting lifetime of variables saves memory space because it is occupied only when the program is executing.

Static

The value of a local variable however is not retained when the function that defines it is terminated. If we desire a variable to retain its value even after the function is terminated, then the variable must be declared as **static.** The value of static variable does not change when the function terminates. Let us have a look on the following program segment.

```
function()
{
    static int alpha;
}
```

The static variable is known to function in which it is defined. It keeps its value in memory.

Illustration :

```
//use of static variable
#include<iostream.h>
#include<stdio.h>
main()
{
    static int begin=5;         //use of static local variable
    inti=0;                     //use of auto local variable
    for(i=1;i<=10;i++);
    {
       printf("%d\n",begin);
       begin+=15;
    }
    return0;
}
```

Output

15
30
45
60
75
90
105
120
135
150

Register

A Register variable has all the characteristics that of an automatic variable. Register variable provides very fast access. This variable can be applied only for local variables.

Extern

Sometimes the size of a program becomes very large and it has to be split into different parts for the sake of convenience. Each part of the large program is stored in different files. If in any of the files, a global variable is declared, there is no need to declare it in other files as well. This will be available to all the functions of the program.

With the help of extern specifier, it can be told to the compiler that the declaration has been made elsewhere and there is no need to allocate fresh storage place to this variable. Therefore the global variable declared in one file is available to other files by extern declarations.

Let us have a look on two different files where File2 is having access to File1.

```
File 1                          File 2
int disc_rate                   extern int disc_rate
main()                          int comp()
{                               {
   ......                          int sum, net;
   ......                          ......
}                                  net=sum*disc_rate;
void remote_access()            }
void count()
{                               {
   ......                          ......
   ......                          ......
}                               }
```

In File1 global variable discount rate (disc_rate) exists.

The discount rate(disc_rate) variable is being accessed by File2 and the net value of discount can be calculated. This is remote access.

Therefore, it is advisable to use extern variable to share data among different parts of a multi-file program. There are same rules in declaring an extern variable as defining the other variables.

Storage Class Specifiers

Storage Class	*Scope or Visibility*	*Lifetime*
auto	function	During function is executed
register	function	During function is executed
static (local)	function	During program is executed
static (global)	file	During program is executed
extern	file	During program is executed

LIBRARIES

A library is a collection of linkable files or programs or functions that can be used by the other programs. Library functions are predefined functions provided by C. These functions are very beneficial for the programmer because a lot of time is saved due to predefinedness of these functions and the programmer is saved of writing the codes of these functions.

Features of Library Function

1. *Time Saving :* Library functions being pre-defined save time. The efforts of redevelopment can be avoided.
2. *Fast Process :* Program Development is faster.
3. *Sharing :* Library functions can be shared by different users.
4. *Less Disk Space :* These functions occupy a lesser space on the disk. Only one copy is to be maintained.

The Standard C Libraries

Several of libraries are available which provide file manipulation and other functions. All the standard functions are included in Header Files. These header files are also known as Library Files. Each function library has a corresponding header file having extension 'h'. When a standard function is used in a program, the header file with this function must be included in the program by pre-processor directive include.

#include<name of header file>

Various Header Files

1. stdio.h
2. string.h
3. math.h
4. stdlib.h
5. iostream.h
6. iomanip.h
7. ctype.h
8. process.h
9. time.h
10. values.h
11. dir.h
12. stat.h
13. share.h
14. dos.h

Header File stdio.h

This file is used for the purpose of declaration for standard I/O functions. Some functions in this file are :

1. clearerr
2. fcloseall
3. fdopen
4. fetcher
5. fopen
6. fputs
7. fread
8. fwrite
9. getc
10. printf
11. putc
12. putchar
13. puts
14. remove
15. rename
16. scanf
17. setupf
18. sprintf
19. vfscanf
20. vprintf

Header File string.h

String library is most popular library. Some functions in this file are :

1. memcpy
2. memset
3. strcpy
4. strchr
5. strcoll
6. strcpy
7. strcmp
8. strlen
9. strnset
10. strrchr
11. strrew
12. strspn
13. strctr
14. strtok
15. strdup
16. strerror
17. strcmpi
18. strxfrim
19. strplerk
20. strstr

Purpose of Some Functions in String.h Header File

1. Strcpy — This is used to copy a string into another.

   General Syntax—strcpy(string1, string2);

2. strchr — This is used to scan a given string for the first occurrence of a character in a string.

   General Syntax—strchr(string.ch);

3. strstr — This is used to locate the positions of a substring.

   General Syntax—strstr(string1, string 2);

Header File math.h

This file consists of the functions required for the purpose of mathematical operations. Algebraic, trigonometric and other allied functions are solved with this file.

The various functions in this file are given below :

1. abs
2. acos
3. arg
4. asin
5. atan
6. log
7. log 10
8. cos
9. exp
10. sin
11. sinh
12. cosh
13. tan
14. tanh
15. sqrt
16. tanl

17. polyl 18. sinl 19. hypot 20. fexpl
21. tanhl 22. hypoll 23. fmod 24. coshl
25. poly

The following table contains the various functions used in math.h header file.

S.No.	*Functions*	*Syntax*	*Purpose*
1.	e^x	double exp (double x);	It determines value of e^x
2.	$\log_{10}x$	double by (double x);	It determines value of $\log_{10}{}^x$
3.	$\sqrt{x}$	double sqrt (double x);	It obtains the square root of x
4.	tan (x)	double tan x (double x);	It obtains the value of tan x
5.	cos (x)	double cos x (double x);	It obtains the value of cos x
6.	sin (x)	double sin x (double x);	It obtains the value of sin x
7.	$\cos^{-1}(x)$	double acos (double x);	It obtains the value of $\cos^{-1}x$
8.	$\sin^{-1}(x)$	double asin (double x);	It obtains the value of $\sin^{-1}x$

Header File stdlib.h

The stdlib.h header file consists of a miscellaneous collection of functions stdlib library includes simple integers math functions, sorting functions. There is another important thing, *i.e.,* of text-conversions (ASCII to integers).

Various functions used in this file have been below :

1. abs 2. abort 3. atof 4. atoi
5. atol 6. exit 7. free 8. labs
9. itoa 10. qsort 11. random 12. strand
13. wctomb 14. strtol 15. fcvt 16. malloc
17. realloc 18. ecvt 19. ultoa

S.No.	*Function*	*Use/purpose*
1.	abs()	To obtain absolute value of an integer
2.	atoi()	Integer Conversion
3.	qsort()	To sort a table
4.	abort	To terminate the program.

Header File ctype.h

This file contains the functions for **character manipulation. These functions operate** on characters.

Functions available in header file ctype.h

1. isalnum	2. isascii
3. isalpha	4. iscontrol
5. isdigit	6. isgraph
7. islower	8. isprint
9. isspace	10. isxdigit
11. ispunct	12. toascii
13. tolower	14. toupper

Function	*Syntax*	*Purpose / Action*
(1) isalnum	int isalnum(int character);	To test—whether the character is alphanumeric. Returns a non-zero value if the character is alphanumeric otherwise zero value.
(2) isalpha	int isalpha(int character);	To test—whether the character is alphabetic. Returns a non-zero value if the character is alphabetic, otherwise zero.
(3) iscntrl	int iscntrl(int character);	To test—whether the character is control character. Returns non-zero value if the character is a control character otherwise zero.
(4) isdigit	int isdigit(int character);	To test—whether the character is a digit. Returns non-zero value if the character is a digit otherwise zero value.
(5) islower	int islower(int character);	To test—whether the character is a lower case character. Returns non-zero value if the character is a lower case alphabet otherwise zero value.
(6) ispunct	int inspunct(int character);	To test—whether the character is a punctuation work. Returns non-zero value if the character is a punctuation mark, otherwise zero value.
(7) isupper	int isupper(int character);	It tests whether the character is a upper case letter. Returns non-zero value if the character is a upper case letter, otherwise zero value.
(8) tolower	int tolower(int character);	Returns a character as a lower case if the character is an upper case letter, otherwise returns unchanged.
(9) toupper	int toupper (int character);	Return a character as a upper case if the character in an upper case letter, otherwise returns unchanged.

SOME OTHER FUNCTIONS EXPLAINED

1. strcpy( )

This function is contained in string.h header file. This copies a string into another.

General Syntax :

```
strcpy(string1, string2);
```

One string is destination string and another is source string.

Program

```
//Copying one string into other.
#include<stdio.h>
#include<string.h>
void main()
{
    char string1[25],string2[25];
    puts("Enter the string);
    gets(string1);
    strcpy(string2, strings1);
    prinf("Output of First String =%&\n", string1);
    printf("Output of Second String =%d\n", string2);
}
```

2. strcat( )

This function is also included in string.h header file. It appends one string (source string) to the end of another string (destination. string). The length of string so obtained is equal to the length of both the strings.

Syntax :

```
strcat(string1, string2);
```

Program

```
//To concatnate one string to other.
#include<stdio.h>
#include<string.h>
#include<conio.h>
main()
{
    char str1[10], str2[15];
    clrscr();
    printf ("Enter First String");
    gets(str1);
    printf ("Enter Second String");
    gets (str2);
```

```
    strcat (str2, str1);
    printf ("Concatnated string=%s", str2);
    getch();
    return 0;
}
```

3. strlen( )

This function is included in string.h header file. This function calculates the length of the string.

Syntax :

```
strlen (string);
```

Program

```
#include<stdio.h>
#include<string.h>
main()
{
    char string[20];
    printf("Enter the string");
    gets(str);
    printf("Length of string = %d", strlen (string));
    return 0;
}
```

4. strcmp( )

This function is also included in string.h header file. This function is used to compare the characters of one string with that of the other.

General Syntax :

```
                    strcmp(string1, string2);
strcmp function     returns a value < 0     if string1<string2;
                    returns zero value      if string1<string2;
                    returns a value>0       if string1>string2;
```

Mathematical Functions

abs( )

This function is included in math.h file. This function obtains absolute value of an integer.

Illustration 10. *Write a program using abs function to calculate absolute value of 4792.*

Solution :

```
//This program obtains the absolute value of 4792.
#include<stdio.h>
#include<stdlib.h>
main()
```

```
{
   int value = 4792;
   absval = abs(val);
   printf("Absolute value = %d\n", absval);
   return 0;
}
```

log 10( )

This function is included in math.h file. This function calculates logarithm to the base 10.

Program

To obtain the logarithm to the base 10 of a given number x. Value of x can be placed as 61.3083

Solution :

```
//This program calculates the logarithm to the
//base 10 of given number x.
#include<stdio.h>
#include<stdlib.h>
#include<math.h>
main()
{
    double x,r;
    x = 61.3083;
    r = log(x);
    printf ("The log to the base 10 = %F\n",r);
    return 0;
}
```

pow( )

This function is included in math.h file. This function calculates the value of expression of the form of x^y.

Program

Develop a program using pow function to obtain the value of x^y.

Take $x = 2.5$

$y = 10$

Solution :

```
//This program uses pow() function to obtain the value of xY
#include<stdio.h>
#include<stdlib.h>
#include<math.h>
main()
{
    float x,y,z;
    x = 2.5;
    y = 10;
```

```
    z = pow(x,y);
    printf("Power = %f\n",z);
    return 0;
}
```

Run

Power = 9536.743164

sqrt()

This function of math.h header file obtains the square root of the number.

Program

Using sqrt function, develop a program to obtain the value of 1577.12.

Solution :

```
//This program calculates the sqrt of a given number.
#include<stdio.h>
#include<stdlib.h>
#include<math.h>
main()
{
    float x,y;
    x = 1577.12;
    y = sqrt(x);
    printf("Square Root = %f\n",y);
    return 0;
}
```

Run

Square Root = 39.712971

sin()

This function of math.h header file calculates the sine of the angle.

cos()

This function of math.h header file calculates the cosine of the angle.

MORE WORKED-OUT EXAMPLES

Example 1. *Write a program to solve a factorial using Recursion.*

Solution :

```
//This program calculates the factorial of the given number using Recursion.
#include<stdio.h>
#include<conio.h>
main()
{
    int factorial(int);
```

```
    int a,number;
    puts("Enter the Number:");
    scanf("%d",number);
    a=factorial(number);
    printf("Factorial of the Number is=%d\n",a);
}
int factorial(int number) //recursive function
{
    int factorial(int); //local function
    int x=1;
    if(number==1)
    return(x);
    else
    x=number*factorial(number-1);
    return(x);
}
}
```

Run of the Program :

```
Enter the Number : 4
Factorial of the Number is = 24
```

Example 2. *Write a function named SUMFUN(), with arguments n and N, which returns the sum of the following series*

$$1-\frac{x^2}{2}+\frac{x^3}{3}-\frac{x^4}{4}+\frac{x^5}{5}-\frac{x^6}{6}+\ldots\ldots\frac{x^N}{N}$$

Solution :

```
SUMFUN(int n,int N)
{
    float x=1,series=1;
    for(int i=2;i<=N;i++)
    {
        for(int j=1;j<=i:j++)
        x=x*n;
        x=x/n;
        if(N%2==0)
        series-=x:
        else
        series+=x:
    }
    printf("Sum of the Series=%f\n",series);
}
```

Example 3. *Write a function named SUMFUN(), with argument x, N, which returns the sum of N terms of the following series :*

$$x-\frac{x^3}{3}+\frac{x^5}{5}-\frac{x^7}{7}+\frac{x^9}{9}.....$$

Solution :

```
void SUMFUN(int x,int N)
{
    double series=()sign=1,x;
    for(int i-1;j<N;i+=2)
    {
        x=pow(x,i)/i;
        x*=sign;
        series+=x;
        sign*=-1;
    }
}
```

Example 4. *Write a function sum( ) in C with two arguments, double x and int n. The function should return a value of type double and it should find the sum of the following series :*

$$1+\frac{x}{1!}+\frac{x^3}{2!}+\frac{x^5}{3!}+\frac{x^7}{4!}+\frac{x^9}{5!}+...+\frac{x^{2n-1}}{n!}$$

Solution :

```
double sum(int n, double)
{
    int i, fact=1. s=1, a=1,j;
    for(i=1;i<=n;i++)
    {
        for(j=1;j<=i;j++)
    {
        fact=fact*j;
    }
    for(j=1;j<=2i-1;j++)
    {
        a=a*x;
    }
    s=s+a/fact;
    a=1;
    fact=1;
}
```

Example 5. *Write a C function that converts a decimal number between 0 to 63 in to a 8-bit binary number and prints the binary.*

Solution :

```
#include<stdio.h>
#include<math.h>
#include<conio.h>
main()
{
    int number;
    void binary(int a);
    clrser();
    puts("Enter Any Number(Less Than 6\n");
    scanf("%d",&number);
    binary(number);
    getch();
}
void binary(int a)
{
    int i,m[10];
    for(i=8;i>=1;i--)
    {
        m[i]=a%2;
        a=a/2;
    }
    for(i=1;i<=8;i++)
    printf(m[i]);
}
```

Example 6. *Write a function* ***seqsum*** *in C with two arguments, double x and int n. The function should return a value of type double and it should find the sum of the following series :*

$$1+\frac{x}{2!}+\frac{x^2}{4!}+\frac{x^3}{6!}+\frac{x^4}{8!}+\frac{x^5}{10!}+...+\frac{x^n}{(2n)!}$$

Solution :

```
//This program finds the sum of series.
#include<stdio.h>
#include<math.h>
float seqsum(double x,int n);
float fact(int m);
void main()
{
    double x;
    int n;
    puts("Enter value of x:");
    scanf("%F",&x);
    puts("Enter value of n:");
    scanf("%d",&x);
```

```
    printf(seqsum(x,n);
}
float seqsum(double x,int n)
{
    float sum=1;
    int i;
    for(i=1;i<=n;i++)
    sum +=pow(x,i)/fact(i+1);
    return sum;
}
float fact(int m)
{
    int i,a=1;
    for(i=1;i<=m;i++)
    a*=i;
    return a;
}
```

Output of the Program :

```
Enter value of x : 5
Enter value of x : 1
3.5
```

Example 7. *Write a C function having two parameters u and n with a type float to find the sum of series guess below :*

$$1-u+\frac{1}{2!}u-\frac{1}{3!}u+\frac{1}{4!}u-\frac{1}{5!}u+....+\frac{1}{n!}u.$$

Solution :

```
#include<stdio.h>
#include<math.h>
#include<conio.h>
long Fact(int i)
float Sum (float U, int n);
void main (void)
{
    float U, Result;
    int n;
    clrscr();
    puts ("Enter U:");
    scanf(%f",&U);
    puts("Enter n:");
    scanf("%d", &n);
    Result = Sum(U,n);
    printf("Result =");
    getch();
}
```

```
long fact(int i)
{
    if(i==0)
    return(1);
    else
    return(i*fact(i-1));
}
float sum (float U,int n)
{
    float S = 0;
    int j;
    int K=1;
    for(j=0;j<=n;j++)
    {
    S+=U/Fact(j)*K;
    K=-K;
    }
    return(S);
}
```

❑❑❑

Chapter

Arrays in C

AN ARRAY

An Array is a data structure and fixed-sized collection of finite number of objects, data values that are of the same type. An array is a collection of data storage locations. Each of the loactions holds the same type of data. The storage location is called an element or component of the array. The individual element within the array is called **subscript**. The subscript is the number of elements in the array surrounded by square brackets[ ].

Array elements are counted from 0. If there are 25 elements, they would be numbered from [0] to [24]. These elements of the given array are denoted by [0], [1], [2], ... [24].

These elements are stored in continuous locations in the memory. Array count starts from 0 and not from 1. The subscript always begins with 0 counting. When the program uses arrays, the array with *n* elements count from Array name [0] to Array name [n-1]. Array name [n] will not exist here.

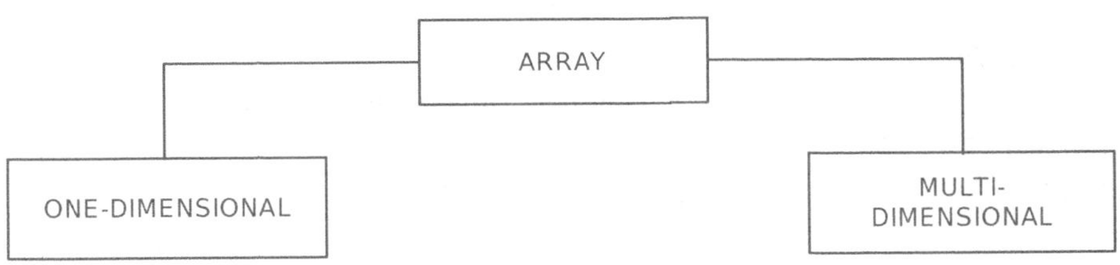

Fig. 8.1

An array may be one-dimensional or multi-dimensional depending upon the specification of elements. If the elements are specified by a single subscript, the array is one-dimensional and if elements are specified by two or more than two subscripts, the array is called multi-dimensional.

ONE-DIMENSIONAL ARRAY

One-dimensional array the elements are specified by a single subscript. This is the simplest form of the away.

Declaration of One-Dimensional Array

Various terms used in the declaration of one-dimensional array are given hereunder :

General Syntax :

type specifier	array name	[array size];
↓	↓	↓
Data type	Indentifier	Size of array

Data type may be of the following types :

int

float

char

double

The following are the valid statements one-dimensional array declaration.

```
int number[25];
char letter[10];
float sum[5];
```

C allows the declaration of more than one arrays on a single line but these arrays should belong to same data type and each array be separated by comma.

int *a*[20], *b*[12], *c*[15];

Correct and Incorrect in Array Declaration Statements

Incorrect	*Correct*
(*i*) int array [-15];	(*i*) int array [15]; Reason : Integer should carry no sign
(*ii*) int number [1 to 25];	(*ii*) int number [25];
(*iii*) float values [25];	(*iii*) float values [25]; Reason : No blank space should be allowed between the array name and square brackets.
(*iv*) int number {array_size};	(*iv*) Array size is missing. Assign a particular value.
(*v*) float int [25];	(*v*) Key-word int cannot be used as array name.

Initialization of Single-Dimensional Array

Initialization means assigning initial values to the elements of an array. Array can be initialized only after it is declared. After the array name equal sign can be put and a list of comma-separated values is written within the braces.

General Syntax :

```
type-specifier array name[array size] = {initial data values};
```

Example

(*i*) int array[8] = {5, 10, 15, 20, 25, 30, 35, 40};

(*ii*) char vowels[5] = {*a, e, i, o, u*};

The program cannot initialize more than declared elements for the array.

int number[5]; {3083, 3084, 3085, 3086, 3087, 3088};

The above line produces a compiler error because 6 values instead of 5 have been initialized.

Reading Data from Array

Array data can be read either by looking or by getting data from each successive element.

Program 1

```
//Reading data from array
//using loop
#include<stdio.h>
main()
{
    int i;
    char array[5];
    printf("Enter Character=");
    for(i=0;i<5;i++)
    {

       scanf("%c",&array [i]);
    }
    for(i=0;i<5;i++)
    {
       printf("Character=%c",array[i]);
    }
}
```

Program 2

```
//Reading data without loop
#include<stdio.h>
main()
{
    int i;
    char array [5];
    printf("Enter Character=");
    for (i=0;i<5;i++)
    {
```

```
        scanf("%c"&array[i]);
    }
    printf("First Character=%c\n",array[0]);
    printf("Second Character=%c\n",array[1]);
    printf("Third Character=%c\n",array[2]);
    printf("Fourth Character=%c\n",array[3]);
    printf("Fifth Character=%c\n", array[4]);
}
```

MULTI-DIMENSIONAL ARRAYS

Arrays having more than one dimensions are called multi-dimensional arrays. An array having two dimensions is called Two-Dimensional array.

Two-dimensional array contains 2 subscripts and

Three-dimensional array contains 3 subscripts and so on.

General Syntax :

type-specifier array name[*a*][*b*] ......[for two-dimensional array]

type-specifier array name[*a*][*b*][*c*] ......[for multi-dimensional array]

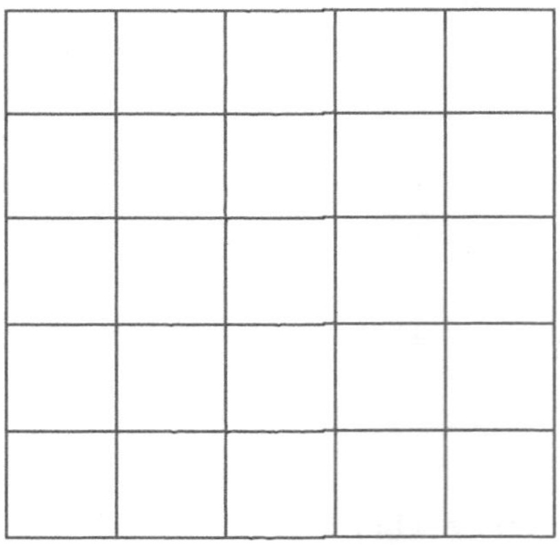

(SQUARE) 5 x 5 SMALL SQUARES

Fig. 8.2

In the above figure, the declaration of array can be

Square [5][5];

This program can also be written as

Square [25]; as one-dimensional

The number of dimensions a, b, c .... given to an array depends from system to system. Mostly one-dimensional or two-dimensional arrays are used instead of three dimensional or four-dimensional arrays due to memory constraints.

Initialization of Multi-Dimensional Arrays

Like one-dimensional arrays, two-dimensional or multi-dimensional arrays can also be initialized. The general rule of initializing the multi-dimensional arrays is similar to that of one-dimensional array.

Syntax :

type-specifier array name [row side][columns]={initial data values};

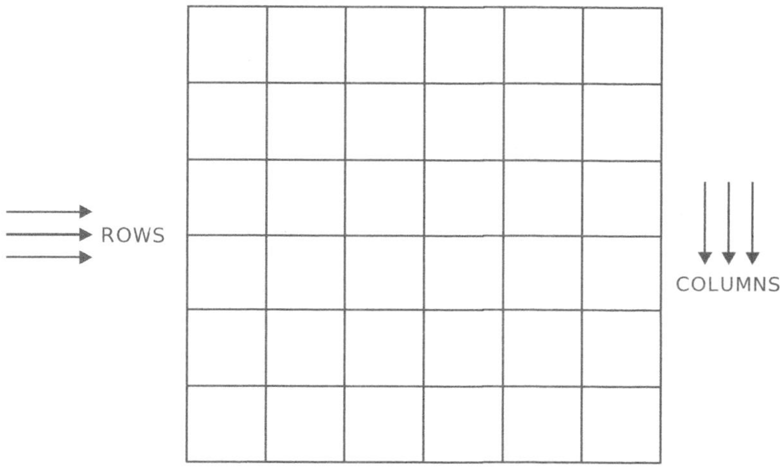

Fig. 8.3

Example:

int marks[2][4] = {10, 12, 13, 14, 15, 16, 17, 18};

For more clarity, the program can group the initialization

int marks[2][4] = {{10, 12}, {13, 14}, {15, 16}, {17, 18}};

The inner braces are ignored by the compiler.

Program

```
//Program to multiply two matrices.
#include<stdio.h>
#include<conio.h>
#define max 10
void main()
{
    int a[max][max];
    int a1[max][max];
    int a2[max][max];
    int i,j,n,m,k,l,e;

    clrscr();
    printf("Enter the size of first matrix");
    scanf("%d%d",&n,&m);
    printf("\nEnter the elements of first matrix\n");
```

```
for(i=0;i<n;i++)
for(j=0;j<m;j++)
scanf("%d",&a[i][j]);

printf("\nEnter the size of second matrix");
scanf("%d%d"&k,&l);
printf("\nEnter the elements of second matrix\n");

for(i=0;i<k;i++)
for(j=0;j<l;j++)
scanf("%d",&a1[i][j]);

printf("First Matrix you entered:\n");
for(i=0;i<n;i++)
{
   for(j=0;j<m;j++)
   printf("%d",a[i][j]);
   printf("\n");
}

printf("Second Matrix you entered:\n");
for(i=0;i<k;i++)
{
   for(j=0;j<l;j++)
   printf("%d",a1[i][j]);
   printf("\n");
}

\\Multiplication of these two matrix

for(i=0;i<n;i++)
{
   for(j=0;j<k;j++)
   {
      a2[i][j]=0;
      for(e=0;e<k;e++)
      {
         a2[i][j]=a2[i][j] + (a[i][e]*a1[e][j]);
      }
   }
}

printf("Multiplication of matrix is:\n");
for(i=0;i<n;i++)
{
   for(j=0;j<l;j++)
   printf("%d",a2[i][j]);
   printf("\n");
}
getch();
}
```

ALGORITHMS FOR ONE-DIMENSIONAL ARRAYS

The following basic operations can be performed on the arrays :

1. Search	2. Insertion
3. Deletion	4. Sort
5. Traversal	6. Merge

Search

Search algorithms are of two types :

(*i*) Linear Search

(*ii*) Binary Search

Linear Search

In linear search algorithm each element of the array is compared one by one with the given item which is to be searched.

This technique traverses the array sequentially to locate the given item. This search is called linear or sequential search.

Consider the following algorithm for linear search.

OBJECT in array ARR is having n elements. This algorithms finds the position (location) LOC of the given item OBJECT. If the search is unsuccessful it sets LOC := 0

The following steps for linear search are explained :

Step No. 1

ARR[n+1]:#OBJECT

Step No. 2

LOC : = 1

Step No. 3

Repeat while ARR[POS]≠ OBJECT

LOC : = LOC | 1

Step No. 4

[Search successful ?]

if LOC = n + 1, then LOC : 0

Step No. 5

END

Illustration 1. *A company has 250 employees working in it. The total number of employees present each day in the month of December is stored in two arrays : DATE and PRESENT.*

Write an algorithm which prints the date on which all employees are present to the mouth of December.

Solution : This given sequence can be broken int 2 steps.

(*i*) Search 250 in the array.

i.e., PRESENT

(*ii*) Print the date from the array DATE when search is made.

Step No. 1

LOC = 1; Flag = False

Step No. 2

Repeat While (LOC<=31)
Perform steps 3 and 4.

Step No. 3

if (PRESENT[POS] = 250) then print
[DATA[LOC]; flag = true]

Step No. 4

LOC = LOC + 1

Step No. 5

if (Flag = False), then print 'Value not searched'

Step No. 6

END

Binary Search

The Binary Search is a fast technique to search the given object in minimum possible comparisons. Each comparison either locates the position for the object (item to be searched) or divides the array list in two halves. Array list must be in order (either in ascending or descending order). The desired element may be present in first half or second half. This technique takes lesser time in searching the element. This should be noted that linear search works both for sorted and unsorted elements. In Binary Search, it is necessary that elements should be sorted either in ascending order or in descending order.

The following figure contains n elements and in Binary Search it is divided into two equal parts *i.e.,* n/2 and n/2.

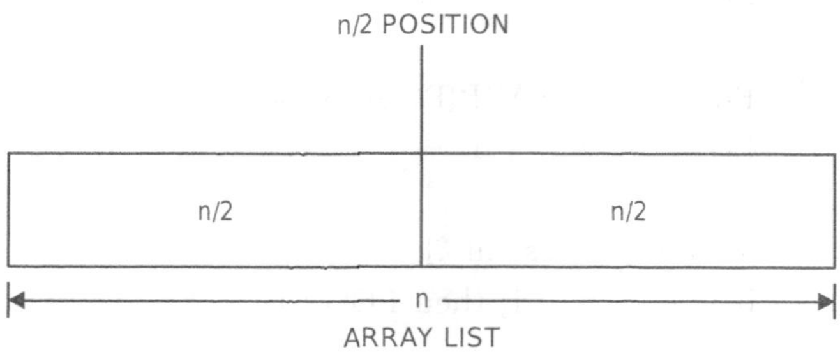

Fig. 8.4

Consider the following example in which the arrays are in sorted form i.e. descending order.

middle element

I

72	61	57	55	53	49	33	28	13	9	7
1	2	3	4	5	6	7	8	9	10	11

In this case n = 11

If you we want to search for element having value 13. The following steps are applied in the binary search.

1. Here n = 11. Binary search begins to locate the value at middle. The middle term shall be calcuated as follows.

$$\text{Middle Term} = \frac{n+1}{2}$$

$$= (11 + 1)/2 \text{ i.e. } 6$$

Now the value of 6th location in this array is 49 but the search is for the value 13.

2. The value 13 lies in the 2nd half.

Now the second half part is again halved.

$$\text{Middle term of second half} = \frac{6+11}{2} = 8.5$$

Now 8.5 can be rounded off to 9.

The 9th element is 13. Therefore the search would be completed element.

Algorithm for Binary Search

Search for location (LOC) of the item OBJECT in the array ARR. LB is lower bound and UB is upper bound.

The variable FIRST, MIDDLE, and LAST denote for first, middle and last location respectively. If the success in insuccessful, it sets POS = 0.

Step No. 1

Set FIRST = LB, LAST = UB
MIDDLE = int (FIRST + LAST)/2

Step No. 2

Repeat Steps 4 and 5.
while FIRST < LAST
and ARR(MIDDLE) ≠ OBJECT

Step No. 3

If OBJECT < ARR(MIDDLE)
Set LAST : = MIDDLE – 1
else FIRST : = MIDDLE + 1

Step No. 4

If Object < ARR (MIDDLE)
Set LAST : = MIDDLE – 1
else FIRST : = MIDDLE + 1

Step No. 5

MIDDLE = int [(FIRST + LAST)/2]

Step No. 6

If ARR(MIDDLE) = OBJECT
LOC : = MIDDLE

Print "Successful Search"
else
LOC : = 0
print "Search Unsuccessful"

Step No. 7

END

Illustration 2. *Write algorithm to search 82.7 in the following array PRICE [5]*

PRICE	52.6	61.5	71.3	77.5	82.7
	0	1	2	3	4
			MIDDLE		

Solution : The given array is in ascending order. OBJECT to be searched is 77.5.

Step No. 1

FIRST = 0
LAST = 4
MIDDLE = int((FIRST + LAST)/2)
= int((0 + 4)/2)
= int(2) = 2

Step No. 2

PRICE[MIDDLE] is 71.3
71.3 <82.7
then FIRST = MIDDLE + 1
= 2 + 1 = 3

[Here
MIDDLE = 2
LAST = 4]

Step No. 3

MIDDLE = int((FIRST + LAST)/2)
int((3 + 4)/2)
= int(7/2)
= int(3.5)
or

77.5	82.7
3	4

Successful search at location no. 4

Program

Write a C program on binary search.

```
#include<stdio.h>
#define true 1
#define false 0
```

```
main()
{
    int  i,n,ar[50],lb,hb,middle,temp,FLAG=false;
    puts("Enter No. of elements(upto 50)");
    scanf("%d",&n);
    puts("Enter sorted elements");
    for(i=1;i<n-1;++i)
    scanf("%d",&ar[i]);
    puts("Enter element to be searched");
    scanf("%d",&temp);
    lb = 0
    hb = n;
    while(hb>lb&&FLAG = false)
    {
       middle = (lb+hb)/2;
       if(temp = ar[middle])
       hb = middle - 1;
       else
       lb = middle + 1;
    }
    if(FLAG==true)
    printf("Element %d exists",temp);
    else
    {
       printf("Element %d does not exist",temp);
    }
}
```

Insertion

Insertion is a process for adding a new element in an array at a particular place. The element can be added in an array very subject to space availability.

The insertion can be done in the following two ways.

1. If the array element are unsorted and are not in order, than the new element can be inserted at the end.
2. If the array elements are sorted and are arranged in ascending or descending order, the new element is added at right position without disturbing the order of elements.

The elements are shifted one step if one element is added.

Consider the following array INSERT having numbers.

31	48	96	112	119	141	149	159			
1	2	3	4	5	6	7	8	9	10	11

Suppose we want to add a number 117 in this array.

31	48	96	112		119	141	149	159	

(appropriate position)

The number 117 will be inserted between 112 and 119 shifting the elements towards right.

31	48	96	112	117	119	141	149	159	
1	2	3	4	5	6	7	8	9	10

Insertion

Algorithm for Insertion

Suppose we want to insert an item OBJECT into the array INSERT at the ith position. Assume that the last element is at nth position.

Step No. 1

Set j: = n

Step No. 2

while j > = i

Repeat Steps 3 and 4

Step No. 3

Set INSERT[j + 1]: = INSERT[j]

(shift the element down)

Step No. 4

j: = j – 1

Step No. 5

Set INSERT{i}: = OBJECT

Step No. 6

Set n: = n + 1

Step No. 7

END

Deletion

The process of deletion is reverse of insertion. In this operation a particular element is deleted from an array. The element, if at the end of the array, can be deleted very easily. The element desired to be deleted is searched by search techniques either by linear Search or by binary Search. After the operation of deletion, the remaining elements are shifted one step back. The nth element copies(shifted) to n–1 position.

the element to be deleted ↕ (39)

PUBLISH	11	22	26	29	37	39	48	53	56

Original array

PUBLISH	11	22	26	29	37		48	53	56

Element removed

PUBLISH	11	22	26	29	37	48	53	56	

Array after deletion

Algorithm

Suppose we want to delete an element from the array PUBLISH

Step No. 1

j: = n

Step No. 2

Repeat steps 3 and 4

while j > = i

Step No. 3

PUBLISH[j + 1] = PUBLISH[j]

Step No. 4

j = j – 1

Step No. 5

Set PUBLISH[i]: = OBJECT

Step No. 6

Set n: = n + 1

Step No. 7

END

Sorting

Sorting is a technique in which the array elements are arranged in a particular order. Simply the order of arrangement may be ascending or descending. In ascending order the elements (number) are arranged from smaller to greater and characters (alphabets) are sorted from A to Z. In descending order the process is just reverse.

20	18	9	40	30	10	19	8	(unarranged list)

List of Elements

8	9	10	18	19	20	30	40	(Arranged list)

Ascending order

40	30	20	19	18	10	9	8	(Arranged list)

Descending order

There are two very common and popular techniques of sorting

(*i*) Selection sort

(*ii*) Bubble sort

Selection Sort

This is a very simple technique and mainly used for one-dimensional arrays. First of all, the smallest element is searched and placed in the first position. After that, the smallest element of rest of elements, is searched and kept at Second position and so on.

Let us understand how selection sort is done.

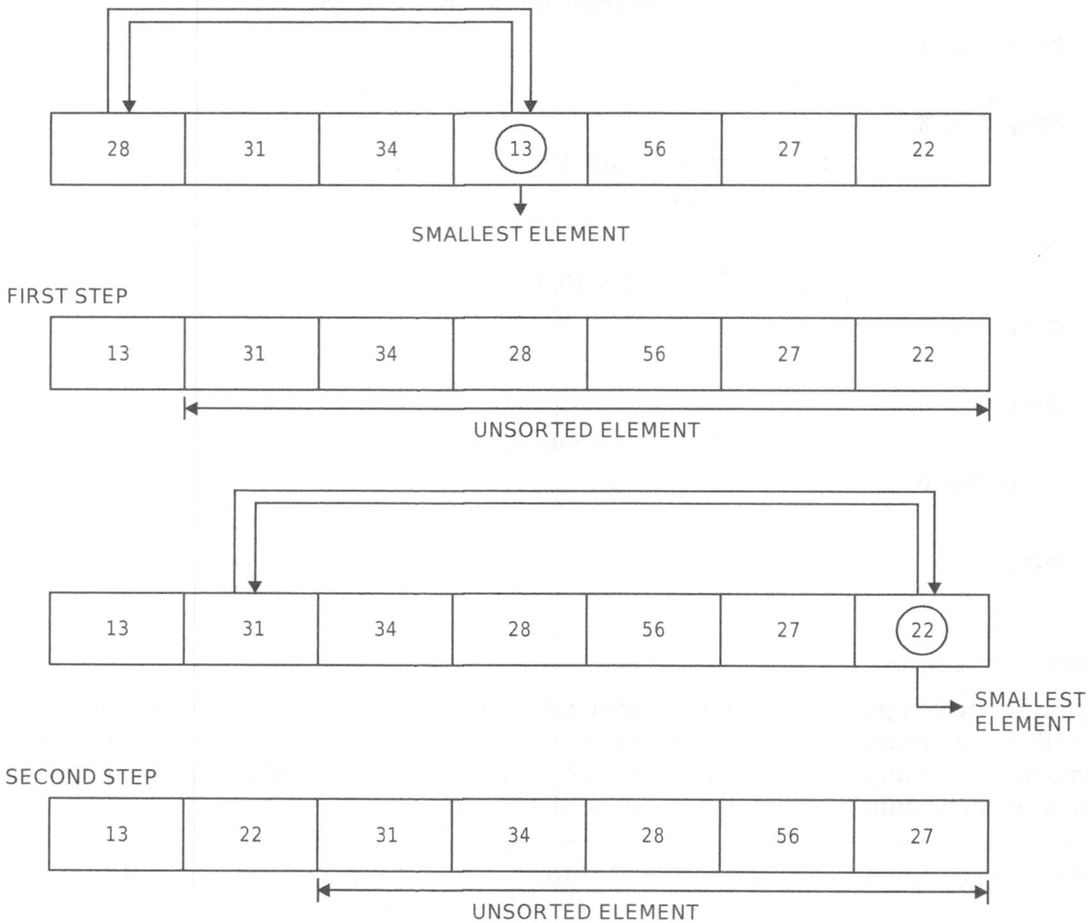

Fig. 8.5

This process continues until all the elements are arranged in an order. Here the order is ascending one. After all the elements are sorted, the array elements will be arranged as under :

13	22	27	28	31	34	56

Algorithm for Selection Sort

Let an array PUBLISH is having n elements and these are sorted and arranged in ascending order. Variables SMALL and POS have been used to locate the smallest element.

Variable TEMP has been used to exchange the first element with the smallest element.

Step No. 1

Repeat steps 2 to 7
for k = 1 to n – 1

Step No. 2

SMALL = PUBLISH[k]
POS = k

Step No. 3

Repeat step No. 4
for j = k + 1 to n

Step No. 4

If(PUBLISH[j]>SMALL)
SMALL = PUBLISH[j]
POS = j

Step No. 5

TEMP = PUBLISH[k]

Step No. 6

PUBLISH[k] = PUBLISH[POS]

Step No. 7

PUBLISH[POS] = TEMP

Step No. 8

END

Illustration

```
//Selection Sort
#include<stdio.h>
void sort(int arr[],int n);
void print(int arr[],int n);
main()
{
    int arr[25];
    int i;
    i=0;
    puts("Enter Numbers");
}
```

The selection sort method repeatedly selects the smallest key in the remaining unsorted array.

The smallest keys are placed in orderly position.

Take the following elements which are unsorted.

9 13 11 8 22 3 (3 is the smallest element in the array)

Pass 1.

3 (sorted part) 9 13 11 8 22 (choose the smallest element and place it in 1st position)

Pass 2.

3 8 (sorted part) 9 13 11 22

Pass 3.

3 8 9 (sorted part) 13 11 22

Pass 4.

3 8 9 11 (sorted part) 13 22

Pass 5.

3 8 9 11 13 (sorted part) 22

Pass 6.

3 8 9 11 13 22 (sorted part)

The array has been sorted in six passes using selection sort.

The exchange selection sort is a modification to selection sort. In the selection sort technique, a separate temporary memory area is required for sorted part. Therefore the selection sort technique requires more space for working. In exchange selection sort, the smallest key is moved into its final position and it is exchanged with the initial key earlier placed in that position.

Let us use the same array for sorting through exchange selection sort technique.

9	13	11	8	22	3	(3 is the smallest element in the array)
3	13	11	8	22	9	(3 placed at final position and 9 coming in its place)
3	8	11	13	22	9	(8 placed at final position and 13 coming in its place)
3	8	9	13	22	11	:
3	8	9	11	22	13	:
3	8	9	11	13	22	:
3	8	9	11	13	22	(and so ...on)

Basis of Difference	*Selection Sort*	*Exchange Sort*
Methdology	The selection sort method repeatedly selects the smallest key in the remaining unsorted array. The smallest keys are placed in orderly position.	In exchange selection sort, the smallest key is moved into its final position and it is exchanged with the initial key earlier placed in that position.
Memory space requirement	In the selection sort technique, a separate temporary memory area is required for sorted part. Therefore the selection sort technique requires more space for working.	Exchange sort technique does not require any separate memory are for sorted part.

```
while((scanf("%d",&arr[i]))!=EOF)
i++;
sort(arr,i)
print(arr,i);
{
    void sort(int arr[],int n)
    {
        int j,k,pos;
        int small,temp;
        for(j=1;j<n-1;j++)
        {
            small = arr[j];
            pos = j;
            for(k=j+1;k<n;++k)
            if(arr[k]<small)
            {
                small=arr[k];
                pos = k;
            }
            temp=arr[j];
            arr[j]=arr[pos];
            arr[pos]=temp;
        }
    }
    void print(int arr[],int n)
    {
        int j;
        puts("Sorted Numbers =");
        for(j = 0;j<n;++j)
        printf("%d/n",arr[j]);
    }
}
```

Bubble Sort

This is also a simple technique of sorting. In this technique, first of all two adjoining elements of the array are compared and if found out of order, these elements are exchanged. After the process is over, the largest element reaches at the end of the array. Consider the following example (as shown in figure)

30	no change	30		30		30		30		30		30		30
60		60	swap	50		50		50		50		50		50
50		50		60	swap	40		40		40		40		40
40		40		40		60	swap	20		20		20		20
20		20		50		20		60	swap	60		60		60
100		100		100		100		100		90	no change	90		
90		90		90		90		90		90		100	swap	70
70		70		70		70		70		70		70		100

Again repeating the same process

30	30	30	30	30	30	30	30
50	50	40	40	40	40	40	40
40	40	50	20	20	20	20	20
20	10	20	50	50	50	50	50
60	60	60	60	60	60	60	60
90	90	90	20	90	90	70	70
70	70	70	70	70	70	90	80
90	100	100	100	100	100	100	100

Again repeating the same process

30	30	30
40	40	20
20	20	40
50	50	50
60	60	60
70	70	70
90	90	90
100	100	100

already arranged

30	20
20	30
40	40
50	50
60	60
70	70
90	90
100	100

sorted array list

The stack, therefore, is a linear structure which can be called dynamic data structures as it can expand or shrink depending upon the size of elements. Stack is an array and it is necessary that number of elements to create a stack as an array, must be known.

Stack Operations

1. Addition of Element

The new element can be inserted at the top only. The insertion of element means pushing the remaining elements down in the order. When the new elements are filled, a situation arises that it is not possible to add any more new element in the array. This situation is called OVERFLOW.

Algorithm

In the following algorithm, the n elements of the array Publish have been sorted in ascending order. Variable flag has been used to show the working of exchange in the Array elements.

Step No. 1

k = 0, flag = false

Step No. 2

Repeat steps through 3 to 5

while(k<n) flag = false

Step No. 3

flag = true

k = k + 1

Step No. 4

Repeat step 5

for j = 1 to n – 1

Step No. 5

If(PUBLISH[j]>PUBLISH[j+1])

TEMP = PUBLISH[j]

PUBLISH[j] = PUBLISH[j+1]

PUBLISH[j+1] = TEMP;

flag = false

Step No. 6

END

The bubble sort, however, is an easy technique, but the phenomenon depends on exchange and it consumes a lot of time when the number of exchanges is much high.

Illustration : *Write a C Program to demonstrate Bubble sort.*

```
#include<stdio.h>
main()
{
    int PUBLISH[100];
```

```
    intj,k,n;
    int TEMP,flag;
    puts("Enter the No. of Elements of the array:");
    scanf("%d",&n);
    puts("Enter the Elements:")
    while(scanf("%Id",&PUBLISH[k]))!=EOF)k++;
    flag = 0;
    k = 0;
    while(k<n - 1&&(!flag))
    {
      flag = 1;
      k++;
      for(j=o;j<n - 1;j++)
      {
        if(PUBLISH[j]>PUBLISH[j+1])
        {
          TEMP = PUBLISH[j];
          PUBLISH[j] = PUBLISH[j+1];
          PUBLISH[j+1] = TEMP;
          flag = 0;
        }
      }
    }
    prinf("\Sorted Elements are:");
    for(k=0;k<n;k++)
    printf("%Id/n",PUBLISH[k]);
}
```

Traversal

Traversal is an operation in which each element of the array is processed one by one.

Consider the following case, in which the elements are processed in the following order.

ARR[0], ARR[1], ARR[2],...ARR[10]

The processing can be on arithmetic operation viz. addition, substraction etc.

Algorithm

Consider that PUBLISH is an array and LB is lower bound and UB is upper bound.

Step No. 1

n = LB

Step No. 2

while n < = UB

repeat steps 3 and 4

Step No. 3

PROCESS PUBLISH[n]

Step No. 4

n = n + 1

Step No. 5

END

Merging

In merging, two or more sorted lists are merged to form a single ordered list. This operation is performed when the size of the arrays is very large. This technique copies the elements of two or more arrays into a new one. In the new array, the elements are arranged in sorted sequence.

Step 1

ARR 1

5	7	11	16	21	30	32	35	38
1	2	3	4	5	6	7	8	9

ARR 2

8	12	20	25	28	35	46
1	2	3	4	5	6	7

ARR_NEW

1	2	3	4	5	6	7	8	9	10	11	12	13	14	15	16

Step 2

ARR 1

5	7	11	16	21	30	32	35	38
1	2	3	4	5	6	7	8	9

ARR 2

8	12	20	25	28	35	46
1	2	3	4	5	6	7

ARR_NEW

5															
1	2	3	4	5	6	7	8	9	10	11	12	13	14	15	16

Step 3

ARR 1

5	7	11	16	21	30	32	35	38
1	2	3	4	5	6	7	8	9

ARR 2

8	12	20	25	28	35	46
1	2	3	4	5	6	7

ARR_NEW

7	8														
1	2	3	4	5	6	7	8	9	10	11	12	13	14	15	16

These steps continue until the new array ARR_NEW takes all the elements of both the arrays.

Algorithm

Let there are two arrays ARR[n] and ARR2[n] having n elements each and these are to be merged into a new array named NEW. Ctr1 and Ctr2 are two variables which show "To be merged". Variables Ctr3 points to be next location in NEW.

Step 1

Ctr1 = 1; Ctr2 = 1; Ctr3 = 1;

Step 2

Repeat Step 3 and 4

while (Ctrl <= n) and (Ctr2 <= n)

Step 3

If ARR1[Ctr1]< ARR2[Ctr2]

NEW[Ctr3] = ARR1[Ctr1];

Ctrl = Ctrl + 1;

Ctr3 = Ctr3 + 1;

Step 4

else

NEW[Ctr3] = ARR2[Ctr2]

Ctr2 = Ctr2 + 1;

Ctr3 = Ctr3 + 1;

Step 5

while (Ctr2 < = n)

NEW[Ctr3] = ARR2[Ctr2]

Ctr3 = Ctr3 + 1;

Ctr2 = Ctr2 + 1;

Step 6

while(Ctrl < = n)

NEW[Ctr3] = ARR1[Ctrl]

Ctr3 = Ctr3 + 1;

Ctrl = Ctrl + 1;

Step 7

END

Illustration 3. *Write an algorithm which finds the locations and values of largest and second largest element in a two dimensional array DATA with N rows and M columns.*

Solution : Suppose FL stores the largest element and SL stores the value of second largest element of the array DATA[N][M].

Algorithm :

Steps :

1. FL = DATA[0][0];
2. SL = DATA[0][0];
3. i = 0;
4. while (i<N) repeat steps 5 to 10
5. j = 0;
6. while (j<M) repeat steps 7 to 9
7. if (FL<DATA[i][j]) then
   FL = DATA[i][j];
8. if (DATA[i][j]<FL)&&
   (SL<DATA[i][j]) then SL = DATA[i][j];
9. i++;
10. j++;
11. print "Largest value is =", FL
    and "Second Largest is =", SL
12. END

Illustration 4. *Write an algorithm to find maximum and minimum values of number stored in a two dimensional array.*

Solution : Let us assume that the size of the array is ARR[5][5]. Two variables MAX and MIN have been used to store maximum and minimum values of numbers stored in ARR.

Algorithm :

Steps :

1. MIN = ARR[0]
2. MAX = ARR[0]
3. i = 0;
4. while (i<10) repeat steps 5 to 8
5. i = 0;
6. while (j<10) repeat steps 7 and 8
7. if (MAX<ARR[i][j])
   MAX<ARR[i][j];
8. if (MIN>ARR[i][j])
   MIN = ARR[i][j];

9. print "Minimum value is =", MIN
   and "Maximum value is =", MAX
10. END

Illustration 5. *An array MARK[40] contains the marks of 40 students in a class. Write a function is C to count the number of students.*

(a) who scored more than 60

(b) who scored below 30.

Solution :

```
#include<stdio.h>
void count(float MARK[40],int &C60,int &C33)
{
    C60 = 0;
    C33 = 0;
    int i;
    for(i=0;i<40;i++)
    {
       if(MARK[i]>60)
       C60++;
       else
       if(MARK[i]<33)
       C33++;
    }
}
```

In the above illustration a function called count() has been used.

Illustration 6. *Suppose a one dimensional array. AR containing image is arranged in ascending order. Write a user defined function in C to search for an integer from AR with the help of linear search method, returning an integer 0 to show absence of the number and integer 1 to show presence of the number in the array.*

Function should have array AR and elements N in the array.

Solution :

```
//This program illustrates the use of user-defined function
//to search for an integer from an Array
#include<stdio.h>
#include<conio.h>
void main()
{
    int linearsearch(int AR[100],int s,int N);
    int a,i;
    int element;
    clrscr();
    puts("Enter Number of Elements =");
    scanf("%d",&n);
```

```
    while(scanf("%Id",&AR[i]))!=EOF)
    i++;
    prinf("%Id",AR[i]);
    puts("Which Element to be Search ?");
    scanf("%d",&elements);
    a=linearsearch(AR,element, N);
    printf("%Id\n",a);
    getch();
}
int linearsearch(int AR[100],int s,int N)
{
    int found = 0;
    int i;
    for(i=1;i<=N;i++)
    if(AR[i]==s)
    return(found = 1);
    return(found);
}
```

Output of the program :

```
Enter Number of Elements : 4
1
3
4
6
Which Element to be Searched ? 5
1
```

MORE WORKED-OUT EXAMPLE

Example 1. *Write a C Program which merges two sorted arrays into a new one.*

```
#include<stdio.h>
#include<conio.h>
main()
{
    int ARRX[15],ARRY[20],NEW[35];
    int j,m,n,CtrX,CtrY,CtrNew;
    puts("\Enter the number of elements of First Array :");
    scanf("%d",&m);
    puts("\Enter the number of elements of Second Array :");
    scanf("%d",&n);
    puts("\Enter elements of First Array:");
    while((scanf("%Id",&ARRX[j]))!= EOF)
```

```
    j++;
    printf("%Id",ARRX[j]);
    puts("Enter elements of Second Array");
    while((scanf("%Id",&ARRY[j]))!= EOF)
    j++;
    printf("%Id",ARRY[j]);
    CtrX = CtrY = CtrNew = 0;
    while(CtrX<m && CtrY <n)
    {
       if(ARRX[CtrX]<ARRY[CtrX])
       NEW[CtrNew++]=ARRX[ARRX++];
       else
       NEW[CtrNew++]=ARRY[ARRY++];
    }
    while(CtrX<m)
    NEW[CtrNew++]=CtrX[CtrX++];
    printf("\The elements in new array are:");
    for(j=0;j<m+n;j++)
    prinf("%Id\n",NEW[j]);
}
```

Chapter

Pointers

POINTERS

The C language allows the programmer to "peek and poke" directly into memory locations. This gives great flexibility and power to the language. Pointer is a variable which can hold the address of a memory location rather than the value at the location.

All variables in a program reside in memory; the statements request that the compiler

```
float x;
x = 7.5;
```

reserve 4 bytes of memory (on a 32-bit computer) for the floating-point variable *x*, then put the value 7.5 in it.

Sometimes we want to know where a variable resides in memory. The address of any variable in the memory is obtained by placing the operator "&" before its name. Therefore &x is the address of x. C allows us to go one stage further and define a variable, called a *pointer*, that contains the address of (*i.e.*, "points to") other variables.

For example :

```
float x;
float* px;

x = 6.5;
px = &x;
```

defines px to be a pointer to objects of type float and sets it equal to the address of x :

Pointer Use for a Variable

The content of the memory location referenced by a pointer is obtained using the "*" operator (this is called *dereferencing* the pointer). Thus, *px refers to the value of x.

C allows us to perform arithmetic operations using pointers, but beware that the "unit" in pointer arithmetic is the size (in bytes) of the object to which the pointer points. For example, if px is a pointer to a variable x of type `float`, then the expression `px + 1` refers not to the next bit or byte in memory but to the location of the next `float` after x (4 bytes away on most workstations); if x were of type double, then px + 1 would refer to a location 8 bytes (the size of a double) away, and so on. Only if x is of type char will px + 1 actually refer to the next byte in memory.

Thus, in

```
char* pc;
float* px;
float x;

x = 6.5;
px = &x;
pc = (char*) px;
```

(the (char*) in the last line is a "cast", which converts one data type to another), px and pc both point to the same location in memory—the address of x–but px+1 and pc+1 point to *different* memory locations.

Consider the following simple code.

```
void main()
{
    float x, y;              /* x and y are of float type */
    float *fp, *fp2;         /* fp and fp2 are pointers to float */
    x = 6.5;                 /* x now contains the value 6.5 */
                             /* print contents and address of x */
    printf("Value of x is %f, address of x %1d/n", x, &x);
    fp = &x;                 /* fp now points to location of x */
                             /* print the contents of fp */
    printf("Value in memory location fp is %f\n", *fp);
                             /* change content of memory location */
    *fp = 9.2;
    printf("New value of x is %f = %f \n", *fp, x);
                             /* perform arithmetic */
    *fp = *fp + 1.5;
    printf("Final value of x is %f = %f \n", *fp, x);
                             /* transfer values */
    y = *fp;
    fp2 = fp;
    printf("Transferred value into y = %f and fp2 = %f \n", y, *fp2);
}
```

Run this code to see the results of these different operations. Note that, while the value of a pointer (if you print it out with printf) is typically a large integer, denoting some particular memory location in the computer, pointers are *not* integers—they are a completely different data type.

BENEFITS OF USING POINTERS

A pointer is a powerful technique in C programming which helps in accessing data by indirect reference.

Pointer plays an important role in C programming with following advantages.

1. It supports dynamic allocation/deallocation of memory.
2. It provides various functions to modify their calling arguments.
3. It allows to pass arrays, strings, functions as function arguments.
4. Pointer helps in swapping the variables without their physical movement.
5. It helps in improving the efficiency of certain routines.
6. It can Access data members and functions.

Pointer Declaration

A pointer is a variable which holds a memory address of another variable in the memory. It is to be noted that each variable is located at a certain location in the memory. This location is called address.

All pointers, when they are created, should be initialised to some value. The value may even be zero. The pointer having zero value is called null pointer.

int *pAge = 0;

Here pAge is a pointer to int. pAge holds the address of an int.

General syntax of pointer declaration :

```
data-type *pointer-variable;
```

The Indirection Operation(*)

Indirection means to access the value at the address held by the pointer. A pointer provides the programmer an indirect way to read the value held at the address.

The indirection operator is called a dereference operator and represented by *(asterisk) with a variable. When a pointer is dereferred, the value stored at the address by the pointer can be retrieved. It is to be kept in mind that *(asterisk) must be preceded by pointer variable as given in the following examples.

```
int *pAge;
char *pName;
double *pSum;
```

The Address Operator (&)

The address operator is represent by '&' and is used to access the address of variable. The & is a unary operator and returns the memory address of its operand. When a variable '*a*' is declared in the program, a storage location '*a*' becomes available in the memory.

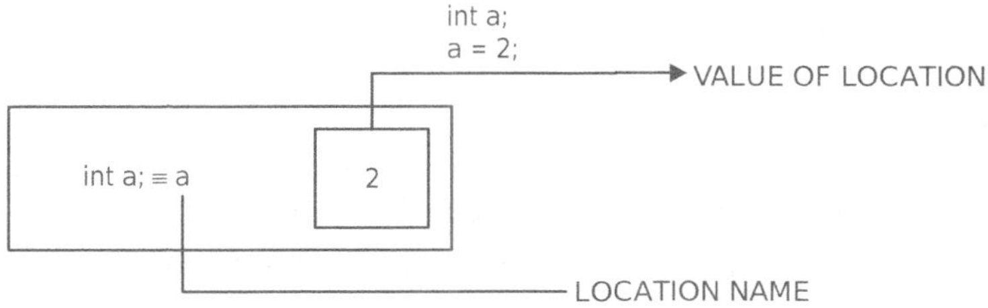

Program

```
//Program to swap two variable using pointers.
#include <stdio.h>
main()
{
int  *a,*b,*c;                            //Declare ptrs
in   A,B;                                 //Declare storage

A = 12;                                   //Initialize storage
B = 9;

a = &A;
b = &B;                                   //Initialize pointers

printf ("%d %d\n", *a, *b)

c = a;                                    //Swap pointers
a = b;
b = c;

printf   ("%d %d\n", *a, *b)

}
```

DYNAMIC ALLOCATION OPERATORS

When a variable is declared, a storage location is created to the program.

int a;

a = 6;

int a; ≡ a	6

When a C program is compiled, the computer's memory breaks down into four zones :

1. Program's code
2. Global Data
3. Stack
4. Heap

The allocation of memory at the time of compilation is referred to as static memory allocation. Dynamic variables can be allocated memory according to the needs of a running program. The allocation of the memory at the run time is referred to as dynamic memory allocation.

POINTERS AND ARRAYS

In C, pointers and arrays are closely related to each other. The first element in the array is numbered as 0. The elements of the array are stored in contigous memory locations. Initialisation is another important characteristic of the array.

The pointer is a variable that can appear on the left side of the assignment operator, whereas the array is constant and it does not appear on the left side of the assignment operator. The difference in the pointer and array is due to this single property otherwise they are similar in all other aspects.

Pointers and One-Dimensional Array

Pointers and one-Dimensional arrays are closely associated with each other. Let us consider the following case :

```
int digit[12];
int *pointer;
```

The array variable digit is an array type. The address of the first element can be declared as digit [0]. The digit [0] holds the address of zeroth element of the array. The pointer variable 'pointer' as given above is also an address to digit[0].

Consider other cases :

1. pointer = &digit[0];

The address of zeroth element has been assigned to pointer variable 'pointer'.

2. pointer++ == digit[1];

   pointer+5 == & digit[5];

   *pointer == digit[ ];

```
//Dynamic allocation of memory for numbers */
#include<stdio.h>
#include<stdlib.h>
main()
{
    int *point;
    int m,n;
    puts("Enter numbers");
    point=(int*)malloc(50*sizeof(int));
    if(point==NULL){
    puts("Memory not allocated");
    exit(1);}
    m = 0;
    while((scanf("%d",point+m))!=EOF)
    m++;
    for(n=0;n<m;++n)
    printf("%d\n",*(point+n));
}
```

Pointers and Multi-dimensional Arrays

The pointer to an array contains the address of first element.

Consider the following cases :

(*i*) &digit[0]

(*ii*) &digit[0][0]

The case (*i*) is an example of single dimensional array and case (*ii*) is that of two dimensional array. Consider the following case :

pointer+1=&digit[0][1]

Here, the pointer variable has been incremented to the next data element.

ARRAYS OF POINTERS

Like any other data type, the pointers may be arranged. All the rules which are applicable to a simple array are applicable to the array of pointers. An array of the pointer contains a collection of address likewise a pointer variable.

Consider the following example :

int *pointer[6];

means

pointer[0]pointer[1]...pointer[6]

Array Pointer

0	1	2	3	4	5

Consider the following case :

int a[15], b[25], c[20];

int *pointer[60];

In this case pointer is an array of pointers which is used to point the first elements of arrays *a, b* and *c*.

Illustration 1. *Write a C Program which displays the contents of an array of pointers.*

Solution :

```
//This program displays the contents of an array of pointers.
#include<stdio.h>
main()
{
    int *ptr[3];              //array of 3 int pointers declared
    int a, b, c;
    a = 6;
    b = 1;
    c = 30;
    ptr[0] = &a;
    ptr[1] = &b;
    ptr[2] = &c;
    for(int j = 0;j<3;j++)
    printf ("The contents of the pointer are : %d\n",ptr[j]);
}
```

Illustration 2.

```
//Inputting and outputting two-dimensional array by pointers
#include <stdio.h>
main()
{
    int number [4][5];
    int *point[4];
    int m,n;
    for(m=0; m<4;++m)
    point[m] = number[m];
    puts("Enter 20 int numbers");
    for(m = 0;m<4;++m)
    for(n=0;n<5;++n)
    scanf("%d",point[m]+n);
    for(m=0;m<4;++m)
    {
       for(n=0;n<5;++n)
       printf("%6d",number[m][n]);
       printf("\n");
    }
    printf("\n");
    for(m=0;m<4;++m)
    {
       for
       (n=0;n<5;++n)
       printf("%6d",*(number[m]+n));
       printf("\n");
    }
    printf("\n");
    for(m=0;m<4;++m)
    {
       for(n=0;n<5;++n)
       printf("%6d",*(pointer[m]+n));
       printf("\n");
    }
    printf("\n");
    for(m=0;m<4;++m)
    {
       for(n=4;n>=0;n--n)
       printf("%6d",*(point[m]+n));
       printf("\n");
    }
}
```

Illustration 3. *This program illustrates the use of pointer variables in handling one-dimensional and multi-dimensional arrays.*

```
//Demonstrates use of string pointers
#include<stdio.h>
#include<string.h>
main()
{
    char *string1 = "LOVE";
    char *string2[5] = {
    "child",
    "boy",
    "girl",
    "man"
    "woman"
    };
    int m,n;
    puts("Case1 :Printing a string");
    printf("%c/n",*string1);
    printf("%s/n",*string1);
    printf("%s/n",*string1+1);
    printf("%s/n",*string1+2);
    for(m=0;m<strlen(string1);++m)
    print("%c\n",*(string1+m));
    printf("\n");
    puts("n\n");
    puts("Case2 :Printing a series of strings");
    for(m=0;m<5;++m)
    printf("%c\n",*string2[m]);
    for(m=0;m<5;++m)
    printf("%s\n",*(string2+m));
    printf("\n");
    for(m=0;m<5;++m)
    {
       for(n=0;n<strlen(string2[m];++n)
       printf("%c",*(string2[m]+n));
       printf("%s","\n");
    }
}
```

POINTERS AND STRINGS

A string is a one dimensional array of characters. A string is terminated by null character *i.e.,* '\θ'. String is written in double quotes.

By using pointers, we can compare, concatenate, copy strings.

Program

```
#include<stdio.h>
void main()
{
    char str[25]="Computer";
    pass(&str[0]);
}
void pass(char * ptr)
{
    while (*ptr!='\0')
    {
        printf("%c",*ptr);
        printf;
    }
}
```

Output

```
Computer
```

MORE WORKED-OUT EXAMPLES

Example 1. *What is the output of the following program ?*

```
void strfunc(char *s)
{
    char *n="Dylan";
    *s=n;}
    void main()
    {
        char *str="Dylan";
        *s=n;}
        void main()
        {
            char *str=Lennon";
            strfunc(&str);
            printf("%c\n",str);
        }
    }
}
```

Solution :

Dylan.

Example 2. *What is the output of the following program ?*

```
#include<stdio.h>
main()
{
   int a=32;
   int *ptr=&a;
   char ch = 'A';
   char *cho=&ch;
   cho +=a;
   *ptr +=ch;
   printf ("%c\n",ch);
}
```

Solution :

```
97A
```

Example 3. *What will be the output of the following program?*

```
#include<stdio.h>
#include<string.h>
void stringfunc(char *str)
{
   int i,j len=strlen(str);
   for (i=0;i<len;i++)
   {
      for(j=0;j<=i;j++)
      printf("Output is % d\n",str[j]);
   }
}
void main()
{
   stringfunc("COMPUTER");
}
```

Solution :

```
Output is
          C
          CO
          COM
          COMP
          COMPU
          COMPUT
          COMPUTE
          COMPUTER
```

DYNAMIC MEMORY ALLOCATION

The memory usage for program data can increase or decrease as your program runs.

The function `malloc()`, `free()`, `calloc()` and `realloc()` give you the power to dynamically allocate memory for your variable at run time.

All these functions reside in `stdlib.h` header file, therefore, do not forget to include the `stdlib.h` header file in your programs.

malloc( ) and free( )

The `malloc()` function requires one argument—the number of bytes you want to allocate dynamically.

Syntax

```
voild *malloc(size_t size);
```

Upon successful allocation, `malloc()` returns a void pointer `(void *)`, which indicates you can assign to a pointer variable, which will store the address of the allocated memory.

If memory allocation failed (for example, if you're out of memory), `malloc()` will return a NULL pointer.

Passing the pointer into `free()` release the allocated memory.

The following example ask you to store integers then allocate the memory dynamically using `malloc()` and store a certain number of integers, print them and releases the used memory using `free()`.

Program

```
#include<stdio.h>
#include<stdlib.h>
   int main() {
   int number;
   int *ptr;
   int i;
   printf("How many integers would you like store? ");
   scanf("%d", &number);
   ptr = malloc(number*sizeof(int)); /* allocating memory */
   if(ptr!=NULL) {
      for(i=0 ; i<number ; i++) {
         *(ptr+i) = i;
      }
         for(i=number; i>0; i--) {
         printf("%d\n", *(ptr+(i-1))); }
         free(ptr);  /* free allocated memory */
         return 0;
   }
   else (
      printf("\nMemory Allocation Failed!! Not Enough Memory!!\n");
```

```
        return 1;
      }
    }
```

Calloc( )

`calloc()` is similar to `malloc()`, but the main difference is that the values stored in the allocated memory space is zero by default. With `malloc()`, the allocated memory could have any vlaue.

Syntax :

```
void *calloc(size_t nvariables, size_t variableSize);
```

`calloc()` requires two arguments. The first is the number of variables for which you have to allocate memory. The second is the size of each variable.

Like `malloc()`, `calloc()` will return a `void` pointer if the memory allocation is successful, otherwise return a NULL pointer.

This example shows how to call `calloc()`.

Program

```
#include<stdio.h>
#include<stdlib.h>
int main() {
   float *calloc1, *calloc2, *malloc1, *malloc2;
   int i;
   calloc1=calloc(2,sizeof(float));
   calloc2=calloc(2,sizeof(float));
   malloc1=malloc(2*sizeof(float));
   malloc2=malloc(2*sizeof(float));
   if(calloc1!=NULL && calloc2!=NULL & malloc1!=NULL && malloc2!=NULL)
   {
      for(i=0 ; i<3 ; i++) {
         printf("calloc1[%d] holds %f,",i,calloc1[i]);
         printf("malloc1[%d] holds %f\n",i,malloc1[i]);
         printf("calloc2[%d] holds %f,",i,*(calloc2+i));
         printf("malloc2[%d] holds %f\n",i,*(malloc2+i));
   }
   free(calloc1);
   free(calloc2);
   free(malloc1);
   free(malloc2);
   return 0;
}
else {
   printf("Not enough memory\n");
```

```
    return 1;
}
getch();
}
```

The calloc1 and calloc2 arrays should hold zeros. Contents of the malloc1 and malloc2 arrays will vary.

realloc( )

Suppose you have allocated a certain number of bytes for an array but later find that you want to add values to it. You could copy everything into a larger array, which is inefficient, or you can allocate more bytes using realloc(), without losing your data.

```
void *realloc(void *pointer, size_t size);
```

realloc() takes two arguments. The first is the pointer referencing the memory. The second is the total number of bytes you want to reallocate.

realloc() behaves like malloc() if the first argument is NULL:

Passing zero as the second argument is the equivalent of calling free.

Once again, realloc() returns a void pointer if successful, else a NULL pointer is returned.

This example uses calloc() to allocate enough memory for an int array of five elements.

Then realloc() is called to extend the array to hold seven elements.

Program

```
#include<stdio.h>
#include<stdlib.h>
int main() {
    int *ptr;
    int i;
    ptr = calloc(5,sizeof(int));
    if(ptr!=NULL) {
        *ptr= 2;
        *(ptr+1)=4;
        ptr[2]=8;
        ptr[3]=16;
        ptr[4]=32;
                          /* ptr[5]=64; will not assign anything */
        ptr=realloc(ptr,7*sizeof(int));

        if(ptr!=NULL) {
            printf("Now allocating more memory...\n");
            ptr[5]=64;       /* Now ptr[5] will assign a value of 64. */
            ptr[6]=128;
```

```
            for(i=0; i<7; i++) {
               printf("ptr[%d] holds %d\n",i,ptr[i]);
            }
            realloc(ptr,0);
            return 0;
         }
         else (
            printf("Not Enough memory!!realloc failed!!n");
            return 1;
         }
      }
      else {
         printf("Not Enough memory!! calloc failed!!\n");
         return 1;
      }
   }
```

Output

```
ptr[0] holds 2
ptr[1] holds 4
ptr[2] holds 8
ptr[3] holds 16
ptr[4] holds 32
ptr[5] holds 64
ptr[6] holds 128
```

Before using `realloc()`, assigning a value to `ptr[5]` will not cause a compile error. The program will still run, but `ptr[5]` will not hold the value you assigned.

Pointers to Functions

A useful technique is the ability to have pointers to functions. Their declaration is easy in the same way as it would be for the function.

For example,

```
int func(int a, float b);
```

and simply put brackets around the name and a * in front of it : that declares the pointer.

If you do not parenthesize the name, you declare a function returning a pointer :

```
Declaration Example
   /* function returning pointer to int */
int *func(int a, float b);
   /* pointer to function returning int */
int (*func) (int a, float b);
```

Once you have got the pointer, you can assign the address of the right sort of function just by using its name : like an array, a function name is turned into an address when it's used in an expression.

You can call the function in the following form.

```
(*func)  (1,2);
```

Program

```
#include<stdio.h>
int sum(int x, int y)
{
   return x + y;
}
int product(int x, int y)
{
   return x * y;
}
int main()
{
   int a = 10;
   int b = 15;
   int result = 0;
   int (*pfunction)(int, int);
   pfunction = sum;
   result = pfunction(a, b);
   printf("\npfunction = Sum = %d", result);
   pfunction = product;
   result = pfunction(a, b);
   printf("\npfunction = Product = %d", result);
}
```

Pointers to Pointers

We can have pointers to other pointers. A pointer is a variable which contains address of a variable. This variable can be another pointer. Therefore, a pointer contains another pointer's address.

The declaration of a pointer-to-pointer is an under :

```
int  **pp;
```

where the two asterisks indicate that two levels of pointers are involved.

Syntax of Pointer-to-Pointer

This is how you call the function with a ptr-to-ptr parameter :

```
//function  prototype
void  func(int**  pp);

int  main()
{
```

```
    int  nvar=2;
    int*  pvar=&nvar;
    func(&pvar);
    ....
    return  0;
}
```

Example :

```
int i = 5, j = 6; k = 7;
int *ip1 = &i, *ip2 = &j;
```

Now we can set

```
pp = &ip1;
```

and pp points to ip1 which points to i.*pp is ip1 and **pp is i or 5.

This technique is useful in certain situations where the operating system wants to be able to move blocks of memory on the heap around at its discretion. The following example demonstrates a pointer to a pointer :

Program

```
#include<stdio.h>
#include<stdlib.h>
int main()
{
    int **p;
    int *q;
    int i=3;
    q=&i;
    p=&q;
    q=*p;
    printf("\n i is=%d", i);
    printf("\n address of i is=%d", &i);
    printf("\n *q is=%d", *q);
    printf("\n *p is=%d", *p);
    free(q);
    free(p);
}
```

❑❑❑

Chapter 1 Structures

STRUCTURES

Sometimes we have to process different data items in different arrays and want to combine them as a single unit. For example, the data relating to employees of an organization contain different data items viz.

1. Employee's Name
2. Age
3. Designation
4. Salary
5. P.F. Number
6. Total Deduction
7. Income Tax

The data may be of type character, integer, floating point number etc. All data types are grouped and the entire collection is referred to as Structure.

Graphical Representation of Structure

Structure

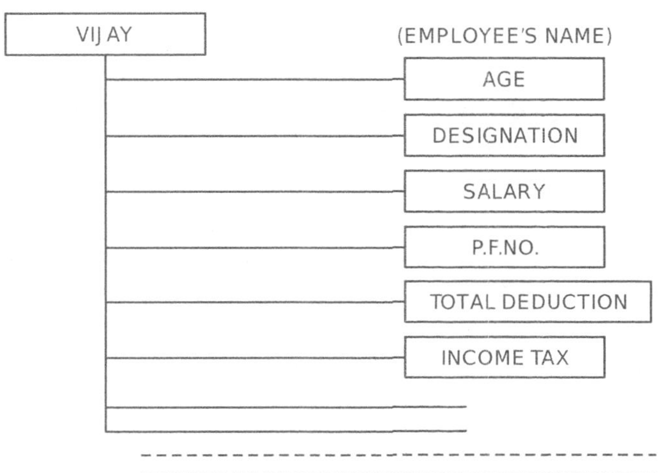

Defining a Structure in C

The definition of a structure is given by keyword struct followed by the user name and followed by opening brace.

After the opening brace, the body (members of structure) is enclosed followed by closing brace.

```
struct user-defined-name
{
    member1;
    member2;
    member3;
    ......
    ......
    membern;
};
```

Based on the above definition, the structure student can be defined as shown below :

```
struct student
{
    char name[30];
    char class
    int marks;
};
```

A structure can be declared in various ways. A structure can be declared in the following format.

1. Combined declaration of structure type and structure variables.
2. Separate declaration of structure type and structure variables.
3. Structure declaration without the use of tag.
4. Structure declaration with **typedef.**
5. Nested structure declarations.
6. Declaration of an array of structures.

COMBINED DECLARATION OF STRUCTURE TYPE AND VARIABLES

The syntax of combined declaration of structure type and structure variables is given below :

storage-specifier struct tag{structure member1...structure membern} structure variable 1...structure variable n;

```
static struct pay           //static is storage class specifier
{
    char pfno[5];
    char name[25];
```

```
    char designation[6];
    float salary;
} accounts, personnel, finance;
```

The structure declaration in the above format may have an optional storage-class specifier, keyword **struct** and an optional tag, an opening brace, followed by declaration of the types and names of the structure members, essential closing brace and declaration of structure variable(s). If only tag appears but structure variables are not given, the declaration is limited only to a type of structure.

There should be at least one structure member. The upper limit is not fixed.

For example :

```
struct play
{
    char player[50];
}   sports;
```

The structure can have an optional storage class specifier or initializer. The structure members cannot have storage-class specifiers or initializers. The following declaration of a structure is **not legal.**

```
struct number
{
    static float n1 = 12345.23;
    long n2 = 45678;                 //illegal declaration
    } integer;
```

The following declaration of a structure is **legal.**

```
struct number
{
    float n1;
    long n2;                         //legal declaration
}   integer = {12345.23,45678};
```

The structure members can be of the following types :

(*i*) **int, long float, double**

(*ii*) array

(*iii*) pointer

(*iv*) structure

(*v*) union

(*vi*) enumeration type data

(*vii*) bit fields

SEPARATE DECLARATION OF STRUCTURE TYPE AND VARIABLES

In this method, structure declaration is split up into two parts, the first part declares the structure type and the second part declares the structure variables.

```
struct salary
{
    char pfno[5];
    char name[20];
    char designation[15];
    char status;
    float pay;
};
struct salary department, personnel;
```

The structure variables **department and personnel** have been declared by using tag salary. We can declare any variable in terms of a tag of a structure.

STRUCTURE DECLARATION WITHOUT THE USE OF TAG

It is to be noted that use of a tag in a structure is necessary when structure type and structure variables are separately declared. In case both the declarations are combined into a single declaration, there is no need for a tag.

Example :

```
struct
{
    char pfno[5];
    char name[25];
    char designation[15];
    char status;
    double pay;
}   department, personnel;
```

The declaration of structure in the above format has certain limitations. Other structures cannot be defined in terms of this structure since there is no tag.

STRUCTURE DECLARATIONS WITH TYPEDEF

The **typedef** declaration is very useful in structure declarations. Tag is not required if you use **typedef.** The structure declaration becomes simpler. The following example shows the use of the **typedef** declaration in the structure declaration.

```
typedef struct
{
    char pfno[5];
    char name[25];              // Declaration of structure type
    char designation[15];
    double pay;
}   emoluments;
```

Declaration of a structure is done in two parts. Firstly, **typedef** is used to declare a structure type. No memory is set aside for declaration of structure type. The structure type in the above declaration is emoluments. Afterwards, structure variables are declared as shown below :

```
emoluments department, personnel; // Declaration of structure variables
```

Another version of the above declaration is as follows :

```
struct salary
{
   char pfno[5];
   char pfname[25];//Declaration of structure type
   char designation[15];
   float salary;
};
typedef struct salary department, personnel;
```

NESTED STRUCTURE DECLARATIONS

A structure can be embedded into another structure. Nested structure can be understood in the following examples.

Example 1 :

```
struct name
{
   char firstname[25];
   char lastname[25];
};
   struct salary
{
   char pfno[5];
   struct name empname;
   char designation[15];
   char status;
   float pay;
}  employee;
```

Employee's name has been taken as two separate names : **firstname** and **lastname.** These names are structure members of structure type name. The key word **struct** followed by a tag name has become a type-specifier like **int** and **long.** The **struct** name **empname** is structure member of employee. Therefore, a structure has become an element another structure.

Example 2 :

```
struct name
{
   char firstname[25];
   char lastname[25];
};
   struct grosspay
{
   float basicpay;
   float da;
   float hra;
   float allowance;
};
struct pay
{
   char pfno[5];
   struct name empname;
   char designation[12];
   struct grosspay salary;
} employee;
```

This example is a extension of the first case. The structure member **salary** of structure **employees has been shown as a separate** structure type **gross** consisting of four components : basicpay, da, hra and allowance.

Arrays of Structure

It is very simple to declare an array of structure. It is, however, necessary to define the structure before an array of its type is declared in the program.

Consider an array which can accommodate 100 elements.

```
struct student
{
   char name[30];
   int rollno;
   int class;
   int age;
   char sex;
};
student data[100];
```

Initialisation of Arrays of Structures

We can easily initialise a structure. The process is as simple as that of array data in C programs. A structure can be initialised as per the following example :

```
struct office
{
   char name[30];
```

```
    int age;
    long int pf_no;
    char sex;
    float salary;
};
    office employee[4]  = {"Pankaj" 29,0061,'M',12455.76}
                          = {"SP Singh" 38,0176,'M',16450.60}
                          = {"Manya" 24,3701,'F',8639.71}
                          = {"Harjit" 35,1101}
};
```

The following values will be assigned to each element of the particular structure;

For 1st Record

employee[1].name = Pankaj

employee[1].age = 29

employee[1].pf_no = 0061

employee[1].sex = M

employee[1].salary = 12455.75

For 2nd Record

employee[2].name = Manya

employee[2].age = 38

employee[2].pf_no = 0176

employee[2].sex = M

employee[2].salary = 16450.60

employee[3].name = Malini

employee[3].age = 24

employee[3].pf_no = 3701

employee[3].sex = F

employee[3].salary = 8639.71

For 4th Record

employee[5].name = Harjit

employee[5].age = 35

employee[5].pf_no = 1101

employee[5].sex = 0

employee[5].salary = 0

In 4th record, two structures have not been initialised and compiler automatically assigns zero value to the elements of a particular record.

Illustration 1. *Write a C Program which demonstrates initialisation of arrays of structures.*

Solution :

```
//This program which demonstrates initialisation of arrays of structures.
#include<stdio.h>
#define MAX[3]
main()
{
   struct office
   {
      char name[30];
      int age;
      long int pf_no;
      char sex;
      float salary;
   };
   office employee[2] = {
   {"Ravina",28,3303,'F',12152.30}
   {"Sanya",24,3701,'F',8639.71}.
   for(int i = 0;i<=MAX-1;++i)
   {
      puts("\Data of employee:")
      printf("\n Name %c",employee[1].name);
      printf("\n Age %d",employee[1].age);
      printf("\n pf_no%1d",employee[1].pf_no);
      printf("\n sex %c",employee[1].sex);
      printf("\n Salary%f",employee[1].salary);
   }
}
```

Output of the Program :

```
Name    :  Ravina
Age     :  28
PF No   :  3303
Sex     :  F
Salary  :  12152.30
Name    :  Sanya
Age     :  24
PF No   :  3701
Sex     :  F
Salary  :  8639.71
Name    :  0
```

Age	:	0
PF No	:	0
Sex	:	0
Salary	:	0

DECLARATION OF MULTI-DIMENSIONAL ARRAY OF STRUCTURES

Multi-dimensional array of structures are very easy to declare. They can be declared like multi-dimensional arrays are declared. In the following example, structure variable **calculation** has been declared as 2 × 2 array structures, each structure having four structure members. The array of four structures, each consisting of four items has been given below :

```
calculation[0][0]
calculation[0][1]
calculation[1][0]
calculation[1][1]
typedef struct
{
    char pfno[5];
    char name[25];
    char designation[16];
    float salary;
} pay;
static pay calculation[2][2];
```

The structure of higher dimensions can also be declared in the same way but they are not usually used in C programming.

MORE WORKED-OUT EXAMPLES

Example 1. *The following program presents an interactive way of inputting data in a structure.*

```
#include <stdio.h>
struct employed
{
    char pfcode[5];
    char name[20];
    char address[20];
};
main()
{
    static struct employed employee[50];
    int n, m = 0;
```

```
    printf("Enter Employee's PF code "Use ^Z to end:");
    while((gets(employee[m].pfcode))!=NULL)
{
    printf("\nEnter Employee's Name:");
    gets(employee[m].name);
    printf("\nEnter Employee's Address:");
    gets(employee[m].address);
    m++;
    printf("\nEnter Employee's PF code:");
}
    for(n=0;n<m;++n)
    printf("\n %-2s%-15s%-15s",employee[n].
    pfcode,employee[n].name,employee[n].address);
}
```

Example 2. *The program illustrates the use of search set convention in reading a structure.*

```
#include <stdio.h>
struct employed
}
    char pfpcode[5];
    char empname[20];
    char empadd[20];
};
    main()
{
    static struct employed employee[50];
    int m,n;
    puts("How many records");
    scanf("%d",&n);
    for(m=0;m<n;++m)
{
    printf("\nEnter Employee's PFcode:");
    scanf("%[^\n]",employee[m].pfcode);
    printf("\n Employee's Name:");
    scanf("%[^\n]",employee[m].empname);
    printf("\n Employee's Address:");
    scanf("%[^/n]", employee[m].empadd);
}
    for(m=0;m<n;++m)
    printf("\n%-2s%-15s%-15s",employee[m].
    pfcode,employee[m].empname,employee[m].empadd);
}
```

Sample output

Enter number of records

1

Enter Employee's code : T101

Employee's Name : Sandeep Sharma

Employee's Address : 1, Shankar Road

T101 Sandeep Sharma 1, Shankar Road

Example 3 :

```
//This program sorts records by using exchange sort method
#include <stdio.h>
struct employed
{
    char empname[21];
    char address[26];
    char telephone[12];
};
main()
{
    static struct employed employee[50],temp;
    int m,n,i,j;
    m = 0;n = 0;
    char c;
    puts("Enter name, address, telephone");
    while((scanf("%c",&employee[m].empname[n]))!=EOF)
{
    for(n=1;n<20;++n)
    scanf("%c",&employee[m].empname[n]);
    for(n=0;n<25;++n))
    scanf("%c",employee[m].address[n]);
    for(n=0;n<11;++n)
    scanf("%c",&employe[m].telephoneno[n]);
    scanf("%",&c);
    n = 0;
    m++;
}
    for(i=0;i<m-1;++1)
    for(j=i+1;j<m;++j)
    if(strcmp(employee[i].empname,employee[j].empname)>0)
{
    temp = employee[i];
    employee[i] = employee[j];
    employee[j] = temp;
}
```

```
    puts("Sorted Records are:");
    for(i=0;i<m;++i)
    printf("%s %s\n");
    employee[i].empname,  employee[i].address,employee[i].telephoneno);
}
```

Structures and Pointers

A pointer is a variable that holds the address of a variable of data type such as int, char, float etc. A pointer can be used for holding the address of structure variable. We can create a pointer to be address of a structure by *operator.

```
struct prog
{
    int x;
    int y;
    float z;
};
struct prog *ptr;
```

ptr is a pointer variable which holds the address of structure prog with three members

— int x

— int y

— float z

There are the following 2 ways in which the pointer variable can be accessed and processed.

1. (*structure-name).field-name = variable;
2. structure-name –> field-name = variable;

Program segments illustring these two ways are given below :

1.
```
struct prog
{
    int x;
    int y;
    float z;
};
    struct prog *ptr,
    (*ptr).x = 61;
    (*ptr).y = 30;
    (*ptr).z = 83.47;
    ____________________
    ____________________
}
```

2.
```
struct prog
{
    int x;
```

```
        int y;
        float z;
    };
        struct prog *ptr;
        ptr -> x = 12;
        ptr -> y = 34;
        ptr -> z = 56.78;
        ________________
        ________________
    }
```

PROCESSING OF POINTERS TO STRUCTURES

Let us study the initializing and accessing of pointers to structures in the following situations :

1. The structure variable is a pointer variable. No pointer variables can be structure members.
2. Variable is a pointer variable; the structure includes pointer variables as structure members.
3. The structure variable is an array of pointer variables pointing to a structure.
4. The structure variable is a multi-dimensional array of pointer variable pointing to a structure.

POINTER TO A STRUCTURE WITH NO MEMBERS AS POINTERS

A structure may have pointers and also ordinary variables as structure members Initialization and accessing of pointer and variable ordinary structure members for structure is explained in the following program.

Illustration 2

```
//Structures and Pointers
#include <stdio.h>
    typedef struct
{
    char firstname[15];
    char lastname[15];
}   member;
    typedef struct {
    member name;
    char address[20];
    double subscription;
}   library;
    main()
{
```

```
      static library *member1,member2={
      "TD","Malhotra","3083,Karnal",10000};
      member1 = member2;//*Initialization of address of pointer.
      printf("%s %s %s %c %d/n",member2.name.firstname,
      member2.name.lastname,member2.address,
      member2.subscription);
   //Accessing structure members through a pointer variable
      print("%s %s %s %s %c %d\n",
      member1->name.firstname,member1->name.lastname,
      member1->address, member1->yearly_subs);
   }
```

Sample Output :

TD Malhotra 3083 Karnal 10,000

In the above program, **member 2** is a **structure** variable of type **library** and **member 1** is a pointer variable pointing to a structure of type **library**.

After declaring of a pointer variable, a specific and valid address must be placed in it to make it legally operational. Therefore, pointer variable **member1** is assigned the beginning address of structure variable **member2** as follows :

member1 = &member2;

The structure variable **member2** has been initialized which is the same as initializing **member1** as well. The structure members have been accessed by using structure **member2** as well as pointer variable member. Different symbol has been used to access individual structure **member1** with pointer variable. The structural pointer operator -> has been used with pointer operator and dot operator with ordinary structure variable.

The structure pointer -> and dot operator (.) have higher precedence over indirection operator (*). Hence we could not use, ***member1.address** for accessing structure member address because **member1** cannot go alongwith dot operator as dot operator has higher precedence than indirection operator(*). To coerce the precedence we can use (*member1).address which will give higher precedence to (***member1**) than the dot operator (.). In this way, we can access structure members with pointer variables in two ways.

1. **pointvar->member**
2. **(*pointvar).member**

The nested structure can be accessed as follows :

1. member1->name.firstname
2. (*member1).name.firstname

TWO-DIMENSIONAL ARRAY OF POINTERS TO STRUCTURES

Two-dimensional pointer variables can also be declared to structures. The processing of multi-dimensional pointer variables is same as the processing of multi-dimensional arrays. Only the valid addresses of the multi-dimensional structure variables requires to be assigned to the corresponding pointer variables.

Program 1

The program illustrates application of two-dimensional array of pointers to structure.

```
#include <stdio.h>
typedef struct
{
    char name[21];
    char address[26];
}   add;
    main()
{
    static add *member[2][2],mem[2][2];
    int m,n,k;
    char ch;
    for(m=0;m<2;++m)
    for(n=0;n<2;++n)
    member[m][n] = &mem[m][n];//Initialization
    k = 0;
    puts("Enter name,address(Twice on a line");
    for(m=0;m<2;++m)
    for(n=0;n<2;++n)
{
    for(k=0;k<20;++k)
    scanf("%c",&member[m][n]->name[k]);
    for(k=0;k<25;++k)
    scanf("%c",&member[m][n]->address[k]);
    scanf("%",&ch);
    k = 0;
}
    for(m=0;m<2;++m)
{
    for(n=0;n<2;++n)
{
    for(n=0;n<2;++n)
    printf("%s %s",member[m][n]->name,member[m][n]->address);
    printf("\n");
}
}
```

PASSING STRUCTURE AS PARAMETERS TO FUNCTIONS

Passing structures as parameters to functions is not much different from passing array or other ordinary variables. Every function has three basic components which need to be understood; once it is done, the other details are automatically taken care of. These basic components are as follows :

1. Declaration of prototype of a function
2. Function calls
3. Function definition

The above components have been described in terms of a structure. There are the following ways to pass structures to functions.

1. Passing structure by value with no return value.
2. Passing structure by value with return value.
3. Passing structure by value and returning a structure.
4. Passing a component of a structure and returning its value.
5. Passing structure by reference.
6. Passing an array of structures to functions.

Program 2

Passing structure by value with no return value

The structure is passed as a parameter to a void function.

```
#include <stdio.h>
struct name
{
   char firstname[40];
   char lastname[40];
};
   void display(struct name x);//Function Prototype
   main()
{
   struct name full;
   puts("Enter firstname<40 characters");
   gets(full.firstname);
   puts("Enter last name<40 characters");
   gets(full.lastname);
   display(fullname);  //Function Call
}
   void display(struct name x)//Function Definition
{
   printf("%s %s %s\n",x.firstname,x.lastname);
}
```

The above program passes entire structure by value as an argument to function.

Program 3

Passing structure by value with return value

The following program illustrates a function that returns a floating point quantity grosspay.

```
#include <stdio.h>
struct wage
{
   char name[30];
   char designation[15];
   float basic;
   float da;
   float hra;
   float cca;
};
   float grosspay(struct wage x);
   main()
{
   float gross;
   static struct wage employee =
   {"Raj Kumar","Director",8000.00,1200.00,600.00.200.00};
   gross = grosspay(employee);
   printf("%s %s %.2f\n",employee.name,employee.designation,gross);
}
   float gross(struct wage employee)
{
   return(employee.basic+employee.da+employee.hra-employee.cca);
}
```

❑❑❑

Chapter **11**

File Processing in C

FILE PROCESSING

Files are the modes of storing data in them. The data tends to decrease or increase in the files. Sometimes their data presents in the files has to be manipulated. The following operations are related with file processing.

(*i*) Declaring a file

(*ii*) Opening a file

(*iii*) Reading data from file

(*iv*) Writing data to a file

(*v*) Manipulating data in a file

(*vi*) Closing the file

C provides a variety of functions that are used to perform the above noted operations.

DECLARING A FILE

A file is a data type which is declared in the following format :

FILE *stream;

FILE is written in uppercase letters. In uppercase it is a structure defined in **stdio.h** with **typedef** statement. There is no need of writing **struct FILE *stream.** The structure members give information on status of a stream covering the fill or empty level of buffer, file handle, buffer size, data transfer buffer, temporary file indicator. In addition, it gives information on status flags. The flags are defined to indicate a wide range of data on status of the file. Definitions of status flags include indicators like read/write file, read only file, write only file, error indicator, **EOF** indicator, etc. In the above syntax of the declaration of a file, FILE is a keyword whereas stream is only an identifier which points to the file structure.

The following declaration of a file are legal and valid.

Format...1

```
FILE *infile;
FILE *outfile;
FILE *payfile;
```

Format...2

```
File *infile;
File *outfile;
File *payfile;
```

The declaration of file(s) in any of the above two formats creates stream pointer or file pointers like **inputfile, outfile** and **payfile** which point to nine structure members of the structure variable **FILE.** Two structure members establish buffer size and buffer area. The stream pointers point to the beginning of the buffer area. All streams other than predefined streams using high level functions use buffers. (A buffer is an area of memory where data are held temporarily to facilitate transfer between devices). It is well-known fact that a printer is not able to print the data with the speed the data is transmitted by the CPU. A buffer acts as storage house of data from where date is flushed to other devices. The predefined streams **stdout, stderr, stdaux** and **stdprn** are not buffered. The **stdin** is line buffered if not redirected. The default modes of the predefined streams can be changed by using the function **setmode.**

OPENING A FILE

A file requires to be opened first with the file pointer positioned on the first character. No input-output functions on a stream can be performed unless it is opened. When a stream is opened, it is connected to named DOS device or file. C Provides a various functions to open a file as a stream. These functions are green below :

(*i*) fopen()

(*ii*) fdopen()

(*iii*) freopen()

(*iv*) open()

```
FILE *fp;
fp = fopen("filename", "mode");
```

The **fopen** function takes two arguments, **Filename** which is opened and with which the stream is associated and **type** of **mode** of opening. The mode may be any one of the following types :

"r" It opens the existing file for reading purpose only. If the file does not exist, **fopen** fails.

"w" It opens the file for writing purpose only. If the file does not exist, a new file is created. If the file exists its contents are destroyed.

"a" It opens the file to write at the end of it. If the does not exist a new file is created.

"r+" It opens the existing file both for reading and writing. If the file does not exist, the **fopen** fails.

"w+" It opens a file both for reading and writing. If a file exists its contents are destroyed. If the file does not exist, a new file is created.

"a+" It opens to read and write at the end of existing file or create a new file.

All the above modes are applicable to both text and binary streams. The default value of_fmode is O_TEXT. By default, all the six modes given above are applicable to text files. If the value of_**fmode** is changed to O_BINARY, all the six modes become applicable to streams in binary modes.

The programmer may not change the value of_**fmode,** he can operate in text mode independent of the value of_**fmode** by appending **'t'** to each of the six modes as follows :

"rt", "wt", "at", "r + t", "w + t", "a + t"

By appending **'b'** to the each of six modes he can get equivalent modes for binary only files.

"rb", "wb", "ab", "r + b", "w + b", "a + b".

If the stream is opened successfully, **fopen** returns a pointer to the stream otherwise it returns NULL.

A few example of opening of streams have been mentioned below :

```
1. inputfile = fopen("input.dat","r");      // for reading-text mode.
2. outputfile = fopen("output.dat","w");    // for writing-text mode.
3. payfile = fopen("pay.dat","a+");         // for reading and writing mode
                                            // at the end of FILE-text
```

The inputfile is the stream; **"input.dat"** is the file, and **r** is the mode and so on in other cases. The naming of the file is subject to all rules applicable to naming of variables. The name of file should not exceed 8 characters and an extension up to 3 characters.

To make the opening of files more general, a programmer may read in the filename and the mode and use them as follows :

inputfile = fopen(filename, mode);

The **fopen** function opens the file.

CLOSING A FILE

After opening a file it must be closed properly. If the file is not closed, data written on the file will be lost if the computer hangs or requires restart. Computer puts an upper limit to the number of files that can be opened at one time. If the files are more than the limit, the files which have been processed may be closed.

Turbo C has two functions **fclose** and **feloseall** to close the file(s). These functions have been described follow:

int fclose(FILE *f);

The function **fclose** closes **FILE f.** All buffers used for inputting or outputting connected with the **FILE** are flushed before closing.

The **fclose** function returns 0 on successful closing a file and **EOF**(-1) in case of any error. The **perror** function can be used to display the error.

int fcloseall()

The **fcloseall** function closes all files except predefined streams **stdin, stderr, stdout, stdprn,** and **stdaux.** Opening or closing predefined streams is done by the system itself. It flushes all buffers associated with the streams before closing them.

The **fcloseall** function returns the total number files it closed. It returns **EOF**(-1) if there is an error in closing any **FILE.**

The functions fclose and fcloseall are defined in **stdio.h.**

After closing a file no input-output functions can be performed on the file unless it is opened again. The **fclose** and **fcloseall** functions empty buffers. The following two functions perform this job without closing the files.

int fflush(FILE *f);

int fflushall();

These functions are defined in **stdio.h.**

These functions clear the buffer contents if the stream is open for input. If the stream is open for output, it writes the buffer contents on the output file associated with the stream.

The **fflush** function returns 0 if it clear the buffer contents and **EOF**(-1) on detection of an error. The **fflushall** function returns number of buffers flushed on success and **EOF**(-1) on detection of an error.

Program : *Program way of closing files.*

```
//Demonstration of close and fcloseall functions
#include<stdio.h>
#include<io.h>
main()
{
   FILE *file1;
   *file2;
   *file1 = fopen("temp.c","r");
   if(fcloseall()!=1)
{  printf("%d\n",fcloseall());perror("");}
   file2 = fopen("input1","r");
   if(fclose(file2)!=0{printf("%d\n",fclose(file2));
   perror("");}
}
```

This program has two files **"temp.c"** and non-existent file **input1. The fcloseall function** close the first file. The second file is not closed as it does not exist. The **fclose** function returns value of **EOF (-1); errno** is set to /; The **perror** function displays the message corresponding to the **errno** value of /.

The fcloseall function is very handy when a large number of files are closed but it has a defect. If an error is detected in one of the files, the programmer will not know which file is creating trouble.

STREAM INPUT-OUTPUT FUNCTIONS

The following console and other input-output are related with input-output streams.

1. cgets()
2. cprintf()
3. cputs
4. cscanf()
5. getc
6. getchar()
7. getch()
8. getche()
9. gets()
10. putc()
11. putch()
12. putch()
13. putchar()
14. puts()
15. sprintf()
16. sscanf()

If we prefix the character **'f'** with most of the functions, we get equivalent stream functions with no change in their meaning, scope and return value except input in read from a specific **FILE** and output written to a specific **FILE.** These functions have been explained below :

1. FUNCTION : **feof()**
   SYNTAX : **int feof(FILE *fp);**
   Use : To detect **EOF** in stream. It returns non-zero if **EOF** is detected otherwise 0. Once the **EOF** is detected, use of functions **rewind** and **clearerr** is be required to clear the **EOF**. The **EOF** indicator is also cleared when the **FILE** is closed.
2. MACRO : **ferror()**
   SYNTAX : **int ferror(FILE *fp);**
   Use : It is a macro that detects input-output error in stream. It returns non-zero on error otherwise(). On detection of **EOF, rewind()** or **clearerr** is required to clear the **EOF**. The **EOF** indicator is also cleared when the **FILE** is closed.

3. FUNCTION : **fgetchar()**
   SYNTAX : **int getchar();**
   PURPOSE : To return the next character read from **stdin** after converting it into **int** type. It returns **EOF** on end-of-file or error, character is read on success.
4. FUNCTION : fget()
   SYNTAX : **int fgetc(FILE *fp);**
   Use : To read a character from the **FILE fp** and returns it in int type. It returns **EOF** on end-of-file or error and character is read on success.
5. FUNCTION : **fgets()**
   SYNTAX : **char *fgets(char *buf,int num,FILE *fp);**
   Use : To read **num-1** characters or up to a newline character from **fp** into the string buf. It appends a **NULL** character to the end of the string. It returns the string pointed to by buf. It returns **NULL** on **EOF**.
6. FUNCTION : **fprintf()**
   SYNTAX : **int printf(FILE *fp,const char *format[ar1...argN];**
   Use : To write data given in arguments according to format string specifications to a **FILE fp**. It returns the number of bytes written. It returns **EOF** on detection of error.
7. FUNCTION : **fputc()**
   SYNTAX : **int fputc(int ch,FILE *fp);**
   Use : To write character **ch to stream FP.** It returns **EOF** on error, character on success.
8. FUNCTION : **fputchar()**
   SYNTAX : **int putchar(int ch);**
   Use : To write character **ch** to **stdout**. It returns **EOF** on error and character **ch** on success.
9. FUNCTION : **fputs()**
   SYNTAX : **int fputs(char *string, FILE*fp);**
   Use : To write string to **fp** without the terminating **NULL** character. No newline character is appended. It returns. **EOF** on error, the last character is outputted on success.
10. FUNCTION : **fscanf()**
    SYNTAX : **int fscanf(FILE*fp,const**
    char*format,[address1...addressN);
    Use : To read and formats input from **fp.**
11. FUNCTION : **getw()**
    SYNTAX : **int getw(FILE *fp);**
    Use : It returns two-bytes integer from **fp**. It returns **EOF** on error or end-of file. It is not used on a stream opened in text mode.

12. FUNCTION : **putw()**
    SYNTAX : **int putw(int w, FILE*fp);**
    Use : To write the integer **w** to **fp**. It returns **EOF** on error and **w** on success.
13. FUNCTION : **ungetc()**
    SYNTAX : **int ungetc(int ch, FILE*pf);**
    Use : It returns the character **ch** already read back to **fp**. It converts **ch** into **int** type before pushing it back to the stream. It returns **EOF** on error and **ch** on success.

CREATING A FILE FROM KEYBOARD

The main steps in creating a file from a keyboard are mentioned below :

— To define file structure with a stream pointer;
— To open the stream with an appropriate function and an error routine;
— To input data from the keyboard;
— To output data to an output file;
— To perform error routine on inputting and outputting; and
— To close file at the end-of-file after performing the error checks.

Program : *The program given below shows how to create a file from the keyboard.*

```
//To create a FILE from keyboard
#include<stdio.h>
#include<error.h>
main()
{
    FILE *outputfile;
    int c;
    char &fname;
    char &type;
    filename = (char*)malloc(sizeof(char)*30);
    type = (char*)malloc(size of(char)*10);
    puts("Enter Name of File for writing");
    gets(fname);
    puts("Enter mode of writing");
    gets(type);
    if((outputfile = fopen(fname,type)==NULL)
{
    perror("");
    exit(1);
}
```

```
    puts("Enter text to the FILE");
    while((c = fgetc(stdin))!=EOF)
    fputc(c,outputfile);
    rewind(outputfile);
    outputfile = fopen(fname,"r");
    while(!feof(outputfile))
    fputchar(fgetc(outputfile);
    fclose(outputfile);
}
```

RECTING OUTPUT TO THE PRINTER

1. Use of DOS redirection Command

DOS provides redirection of output to any device. The redirection **command** > N redirects output to the printer. The > sign specifies the destination and PRN printer.

Program

```
//Sending output to the printer
#include<stdio.h>
#include<string.h>
main()
{
    char name[25],class[25];
    float fee;
    cprintf("What is the name?\r\n");
    gets(name);
    cprintf("Fess ?\r\n");
    gets(class);
    cprintf("Enter Class?\r\n");
    scanf("%f",&fee);
    printf("%-22s%-22s%-22s%-10s\n\n",
    "NAME","Class","Fees");
    printf("%-22s%-22s$%-12.2f\n",name,class,fee);
}
```

Program

```
//COPYING ONE FILE TO ANOTHER
#include<stdio.h>
#include<errno.h>
main()
{
    FILE *inputfile, *outputfile;
    char *fname;
    filename = (char*)malloc(sizeofchar)*20);
```

```
    puts("Enter name of the output FILE");
    gets(fname);
    if((inputfile = fopen("creat2","r"))==NULL)
{
    perror("");
    exit(1);
}
    while(!feof(inputfile))
{
    fputc(fgetc(inputfile),outputfile);
    if(ferror(inputfile) || ferror(outputfile)
{
    perror("");
    exit(1);
}
}
    fclose(inputfile);
    fclose(outputfile);
}
```

RANDOM ACCESS

The files being created in previous topics, are created sequentially; only access to files may be sequential or random processing from byte 1 or first record onwards. Functions in C dealing with random access of the files have been explained below :

FUNCTION	:	**fseek()**
SYNTAX	:	**int fseek(FILE *fp, long offset, int origin);**
Use	:	**fseek** sets the **FILE** pointer associated with the stream **fp** that is determined by the variable **offset** and **origin** in the following ways :
Origin	:	**Starting position in the FILE**
SEEK_SET or 0	:	beginning of the file
SEEK_CUR or 1	:	current position of the file
SEEK_END or 2	:	end of the file

The **offset** refers to the character to which the **FILE** is repositioned on the stream relative to the starting position determined by value of origin. It is a long integer. Consider the following examples.

fseek(infile,0L,0);	Move to the beginning of the FILE
fseek(infile,0L,2);	Move to the end of the FILE
fseek(infile,5L,1);	Move 5 character ahead from the current position of the FILE
fseek(infile,-8L,1);	Move back 8 character from the current position of the FILE
fseek(infile,-9L,2);	Go back 9 characters from the end of the FILE

Use of **fseek()** should be followed by input or output operation. It returns () on success and non-zero on non-success. Its prototype type is given in **stdio.h.**

FUNCTION : **ftell()**

SYNTAX : **long int ftell(FILE *fp);**

Use : It returns the offset value of the current pointer for **fp** in bytes from the beginning of the **FILE**. It returns the current **FILE** pointer position on success and – 1L on error with positive value of **ERRNO**. Its prototype is given **stdio.h.**

FUNCTION : **fgetpor()**

SYNTAX : **int fgetops(FILE *fp, fpos_t *p);**

Use : It gets the current **FILE** pointer position for **fp** and stores it into the variable pointed by **p**. The type-specifier **fpos t** is defined in **stdio.h** as **typedef long fpos_t**. It returns () on success and non-zero on failure. On failure the value of **ERRNO** is set to the value of one of the following two mnemonics.

EBADF : Bad FILE number

EINVAL : Invalid argument

FUNCTION : fsetpos()

SYNTAX : **int fsetpos(FILE *fp,const fpos_t *p);**

Use : It sets the **FILE** pointer to a new position where the last **fgetpos()** was called. It clears all error and **EOF** flags and also effect of **ungetc()**. The next operation on **fp,** after call to **fsetposa(),** can be input of output. On success it returns 0 and on failure it returns a non-zero value with non-zero value of **ERRNO**.

Of the random access functions explained above, **fseek**() and **ftell**() are of utmost importance. They are important and essential functions which are usually used. They serve the purposes of **fgetpos**() and **fsetpos**().

Function fseek()

The fseek() function is used to process data in random data files.

For using this functional, information on data file, offset value and starting position is required.

Syntax :

fseek(datafile, offset value, start position)

Program

```
//Use of fseek() & ftell()
#include<stdio.h>
#include<string.h>
#include<stdlib.h>
main()
{
   FILE *inputfile;
```

```
    long bytes;
    int flag;
    char word[20];
    if((inputfile = fopen("test.dat","r"))==NULL)
{
    perror("It is a Wrong FILE");exit(1);
}
    flag = fseek(inputfile,0L,2);
    if(flag!=0)
{
    fprintf(stderr,"%s could not be positioned at the EOF\n",inputfile);
    fclsoe(inputfile);
    exit(-i);
}
    bytes = ftell(inputfile);
    while(bytes>0)
{
    flag = fseek(inputfile,bytes-16L,0);
    if(flag!=0)
{
    fprintf(stderr,%s could not be positioned for reading\n",inputfile);
    fclose(inputfile);
    exit(-1);
}
    fscanf(inputfile,"%s",word);
    bytes = ftell (input file);
    prinf ("%s/n",word);
    bytes = bytes-strlen(word)-1;
}
}
```

Sample Output :

Delhi
Mumbai
Chandigarh
Bhopal

Bhopal
Chandigarh
Mumbai
Delhi

Program : *Write a program to read a file and search for a character.*

```
#include<studio>
main()
  {
    FILE *fp;
    char c;
    fp=fopen("advichis.dat", "a+");
    while((c=getchar())!=EOF)
    printf("%c",c);
    fclose(fp);
    long n;
    fp=fopen("advichis.dat", "r");
    n=0L;
    while(feof(fp)==0)
    {
      fseek(fp,n,0);
      printf("Position of %c is %ld/n", getc(fp),ftell(fp));
      n=n+5L;
    }
      putchar('n');
    fseel(fp,-1L,2);
    do
  {
    putchar(getc(fp));
    while(!fseek(fp,-2L,1));
  fclose(fp);
}
```

❑❑❑

Chapter 12

Data Structures : Linked Lists

LINKED LIST—INTRODUCTION

List means a linear collection of elements *i.e.,* elements stored in a sequence.

Arrays are also one of the forms of linear lists. However an array is a simple and powerful data structure but there are some disadvantages of this structure :

(*i*) It is static nature. An array cannot be created and destroyed in program execution. This occupies a lot of extra space which is just a sort of wastage.

(*ii*) Its size should be known in advance.

(*iii*) Lot of shifting is required for insertion on deletion of an element in the array.

The concept of linked lists overcomes the difficulties of arrays.

A linked list may be defined as a linear collection of data elements which are called nodes and these nodes point to the next nodes by means of pointers. A linked list is a dynamic data structure and its size can grow or shrink during the execution of program.

Each node contains the element and a pointer to a record containing its successor. This pointer is called LINK pointer. The last node contains zero and this pointer is called NULL pointer.

Each node is divided into two parts :

(*i*) DATA

(*ii*) LINK

The DATA part contains information about the element and the LINK part contains the address to the next node in the list.

DATA	LINK

(node)

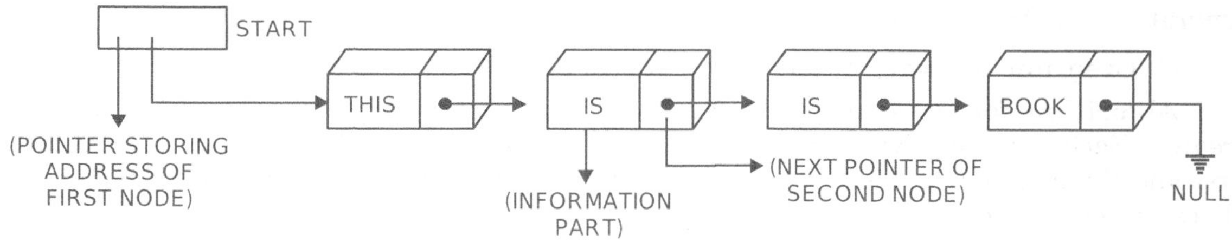

Fig. 12.1

The last node does not point to any node, therefore, its LINK part contains NULL pointer. The information part is written as INFO for the sake of convenience.

Representation of a Linked List in Memory

A linked list requires two linear arrays to store in memory. The first array stores the data value *i.e.,* information and called INFO and the second is known as LINK array which is for next pointer storage. Another variable AVAIL is required to point the next free memory location and called free-storage. This free-storage is allocated with the help of new operator.

Declaration of Linked List

Declaration of linked list is done with the help of structure as follows :

```
structure node
{
   data-type data;
   node*next;
};
   node *ptr;
   ptr = new node;
```

An implementation of linked list.

```
#include<stdio.h>
      struct list {
         int value;
         struct list*next;
};

main()
{
         struct list n1, n2, n3;
         ini i;
         n1,value = 10;
         n2,value = 20;
         n3,value = 30;
         n1.next = &n2;
         n2.next = &n3;
         i = n1.next->value);
         printf("%d\n",n2.next->value);
}
```

Operations on Linked List

(*i*) **Creation of Linked list.** Creation of linked list is very simple.

Algorithm for creating a linked list. In this for a linked list having N nodes is created. Each node has two parts DATA and LINK. The first node is pointed by a pointer first and the last node of the list points to NULL. The operator new is used for the dynamic allocation of a node.

A variable I has been used as a counter to count the number of list.

Steps :

1. If AVAIL = NULL Print "Overflow" go to step 13
2. FIRST = new node
3. AVAIL = AVAIL –> LINK
4. Read (DATA(FIRST))
5. FIRST –> LINK = NULL
6. FAR = FIRST
7. For I = 1 to N – 1 repeat steps 8 to 12
8. LAST = new node
9. Read(DATA(LAST))
10. LINK(LAST) = NULL
11. LINK(Far) = LAST
12. FAR = LAST
13. END.

In the above algorithm, three pointers—FIRST, FAR and LAST have been used.

The first pointer is used to point to the FIRST node in the list. The FAR pointer is used to keep track of current LAST node in the list.

Let us explain the algorithm diagramatically, suppose N = 3. This means that linked list of 3 nodes is to be created.

First of all memory is allocated for the new node (FIRST) as in step 2 of the algorithm.

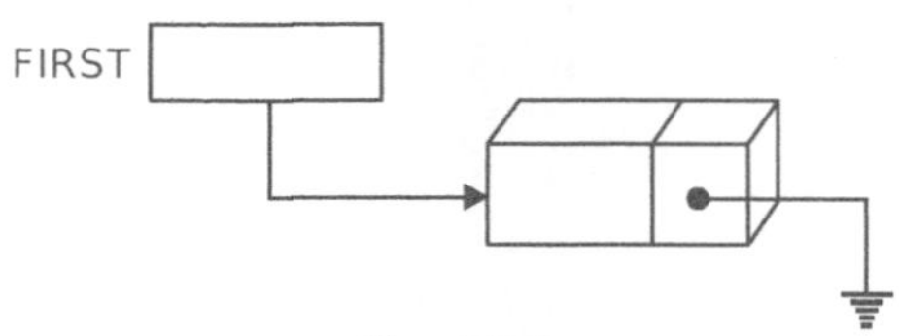

Fig. 12.2

Suppose the value in the FIRST node is A.

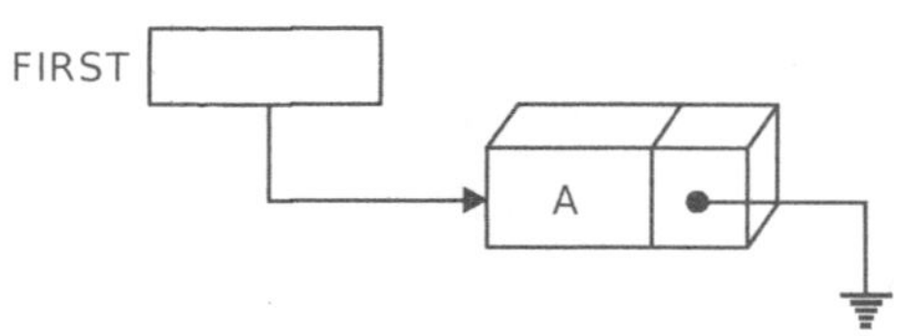

Fig. 12.3

The address of first node is stored in another variable called FAR as per step 6 of the algorithm.

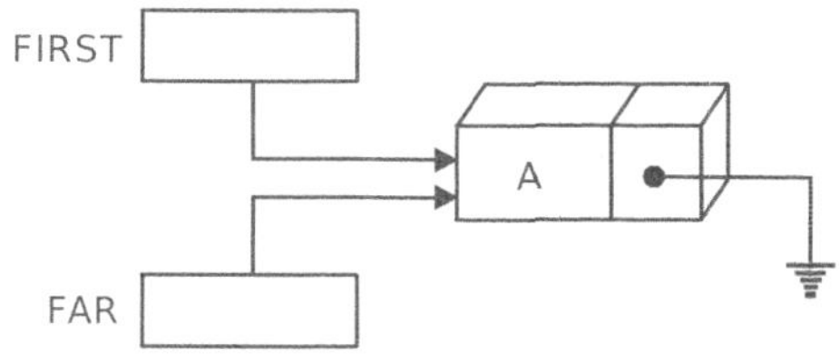

Fig. 12.4

Now the memory is allocated for another variable LAST as in step 8 of the algorithm. Suppose the value in the LAST is B.

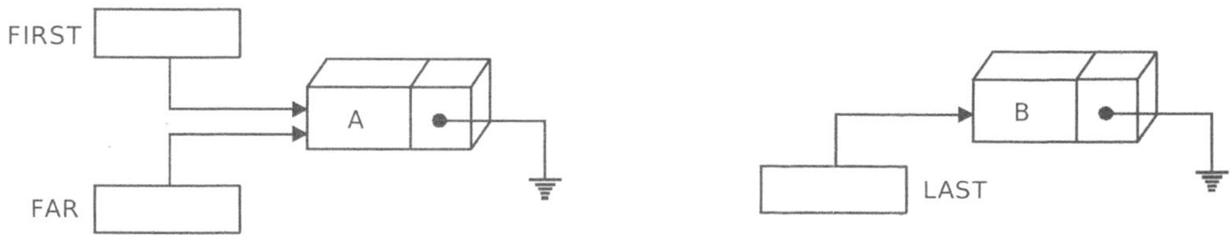

Fig. 12.5

The above figure now contains two nodes. A LINK part is created between these two nodes as per step 11 of the algorithm.

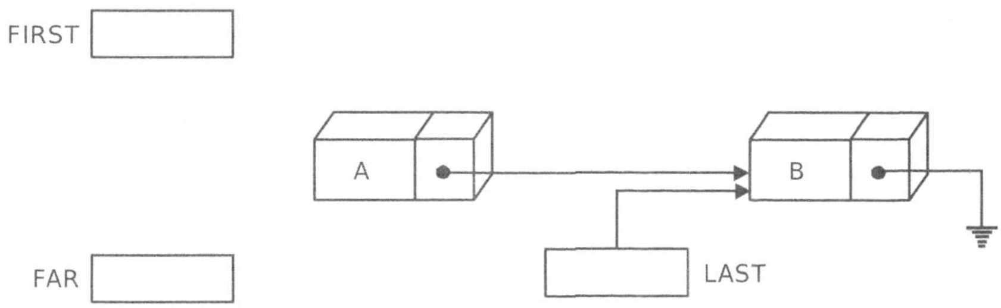

Fig. 12.6

The address of LAST is stored in FAR as in step 12 of the algorithm.

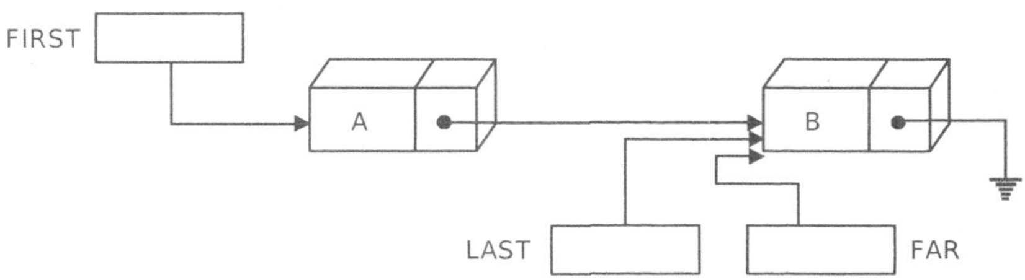

Fig. 12.7

Now, the memory is allocated for another node LAST as in step 11 of the algorithm. Suppose the value in the LAST is C.

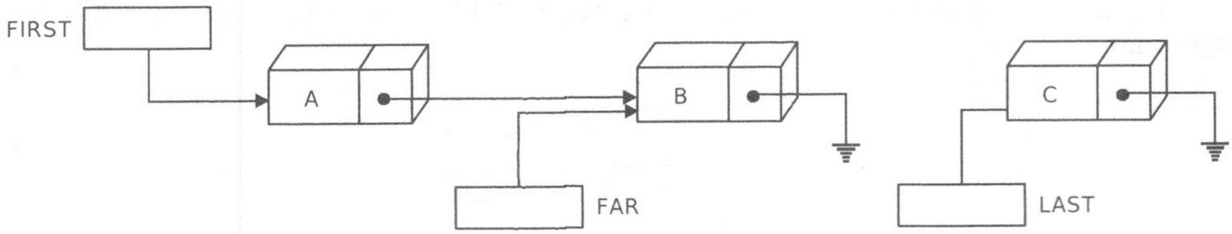

Fig. 12.8

The address of LAST is stored in FAR as shown below :

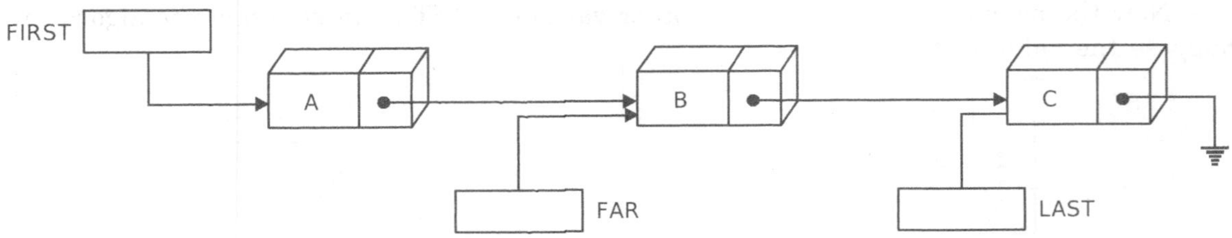

Fig. 12.9

In the linked list of 3 nodes, the first node is pointed by FIRST and the Last node is pointed by NULL.

The following program shows how a simple, linear linked list can be constructed in C, using dynamic memory allocation and pointers.

```
#includ<stdlib.h>
#includ<stdlib.h>

struct list {
   int val;
   struct list * next;
}

typeset struct list them;

int main(){
   item *current, *head;
   int i;

   head=NULL;

   for(i=1;<=10;i++) {
      current=(item *)malloc(sizeof(item));
      current -> val = i;
      current -> next = head;
      head = current;
   }
```

```
    current = head;

    while(current) {
        printf("%d\n, current->val);
        current = current -> next;
    }
}
```

Traversal of Linked List

Traversal means processing of elements of linked list one by one *i.e.,* to visit each node of the list.

Algorithm for traversal of a linked list

The linked list is travelled pointed by First. The number of nodes is counted during the travel. A pointer PTR is used to visit the various nodes in the list.

Steps :

1. If FIRST = NULL
2. print "List Empty" go to step 6
   PTR = FIRST
3. While (PTR< >NULL) repeat steps 4 to 5
4. print (PTR → DATA)
5. PTR = PTR → LINK
6. END.

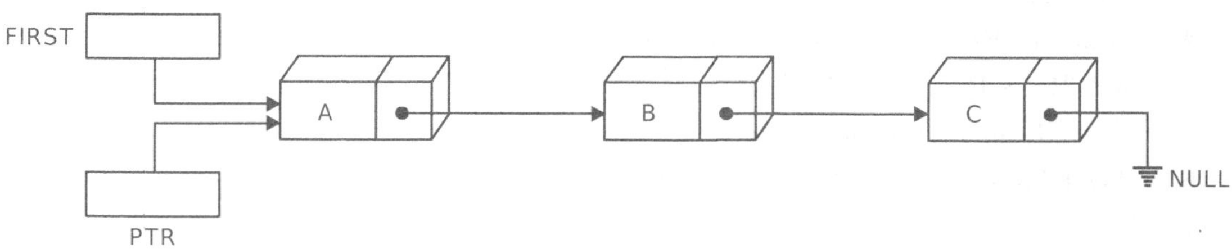

Fig. 12.10

In the above figure, the address of FIRST is copied to a variable PTR.

Travel the list till the end of list is reached. PTR = PTR → LINK moves the PTR to next nodes as follows :

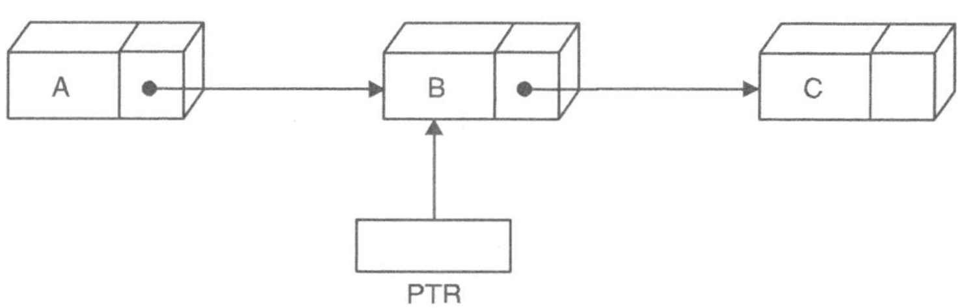

Fig. 12.11

PTR = PTR → LINK moves to the next node.

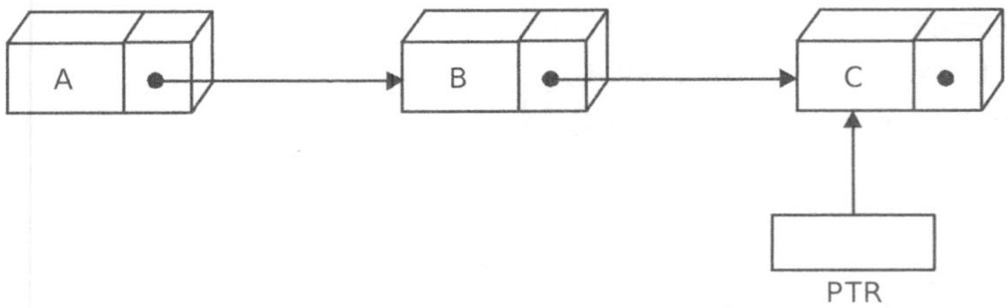

Fig. 12.12

After the above step, the NULL value is reached and traversing finishes :

Searching in Linked List

Searching is an operation in which an item is searched in a linked list.

The specific item is searched until end of the list is reached. This operation is similar to traversing the list.

Algorithm for Searching in Linked List

Steps :

1. if FIRST = NULL
   print "List is Empty" go to step 7
2. PTR = FIRST
3. Read(OBJECT)
4. while (PTR<>NULL) repeat step 5 to 6
5. if(PTR –> DATA = OBJECT)
   print "Item found" go to step 8
6. else PTR → LINK (shift PTR to the next node)
7. END.

Suppose we have to search an item C in the linked list as given below :

The address of the first node is stored in the data variable PTR.

The data part in the PTR is compared with OBJECT. If OBJECT not found in the first node, PTR is moved to the next node with PTR = PTR –> LINK.

This process continues until the desired item is found.

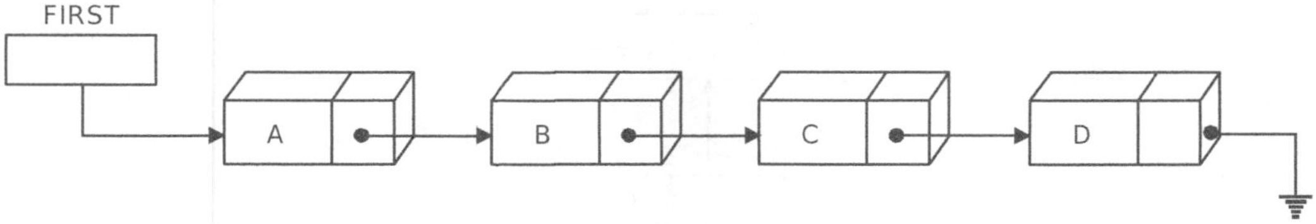

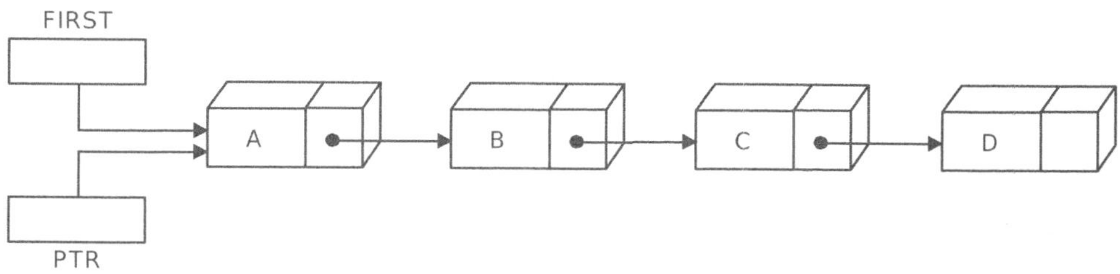

Fig. 12.13

Insertion in a Linked List

Insertion in a linked list can take place in three ways :

(*i*) in the beginning of list.

(*ii*) in between of list.

(*iii*) at the end of list.

Insertion in the Beginning

Algorithm for Insertion at beginning

Steps :

1. If AVAIL = NULL
   print "Overflow" go to step 6
2. X = newnode
3. Read (OBJECT)
4. If(FIRST = NULL) then
   FIRST –> DATA = OBJECT
   FIRST –> LINK = FIRST
5. else X –> DATA = OBJECT
   X –> LINK = FIRST
   FIRST = X
6. END.

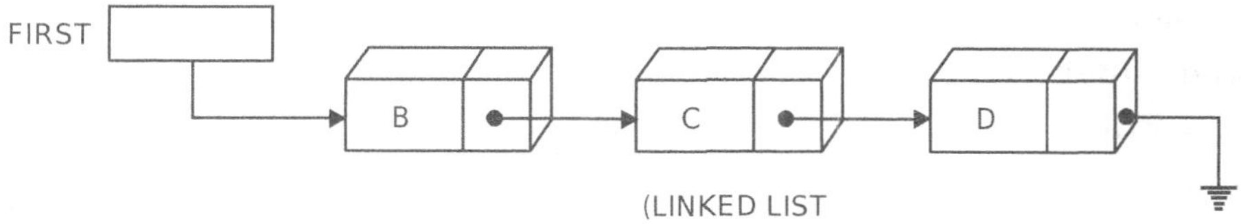

(LINKED LIST
BEFORE INSERTION)

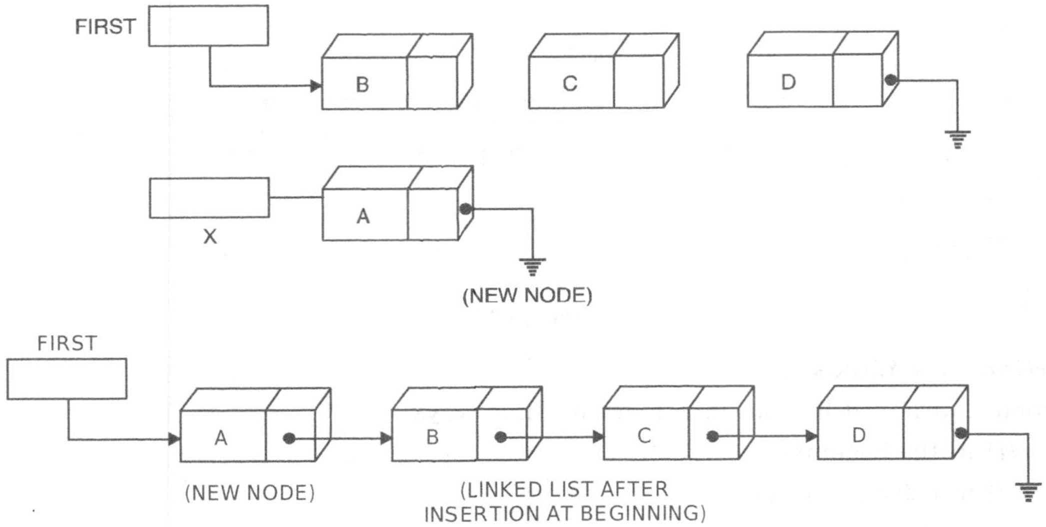

Fig. 12.14

General Function for insertion of element beginning

```
node *and(node *FIRST,data_type OBJECT)
{
    node * X;
    X = newnode;
    X -> DATA = OBJECT;
    X -> LINK = FIRST;
    FIRST = X;
    return(FIRST);
}
```

Insertion in Between

Algorithm for Insertion in Between

Steps :

1. If AVAIL = NULL
   print "Overflow" go to step 8
2. X = newnode
3. Read (OBJECT)
4. X1 = FIRST
5. While (XI <> NULL) repeat steps 6 to 7
6. If (X –> DATA = OBJECT)
   X –> LINK = X1 –> LINK
   X1 –> LINK = X
7. X1 = X1 –> LINK
8. END.

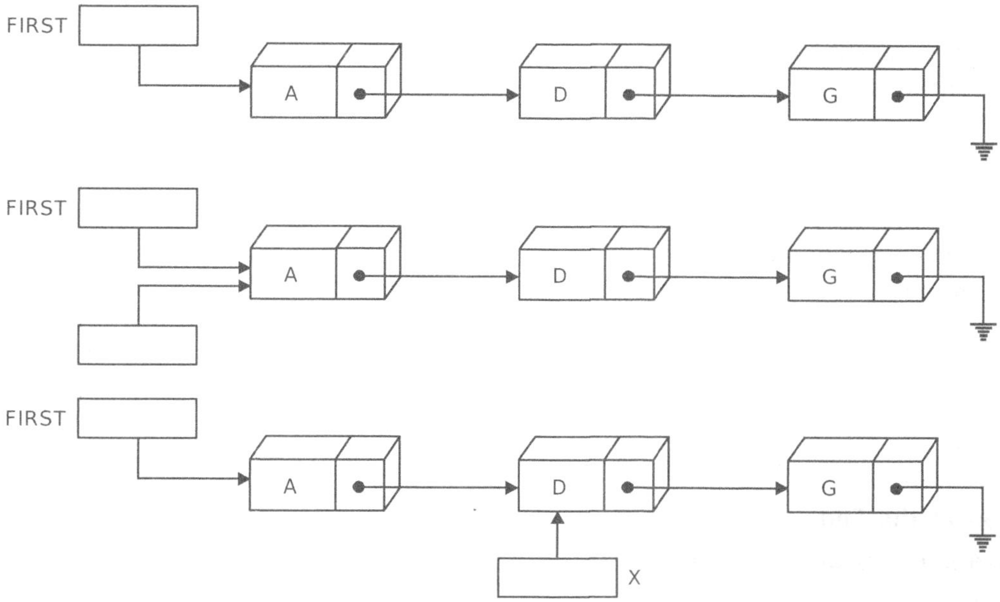

Fig. 12.15

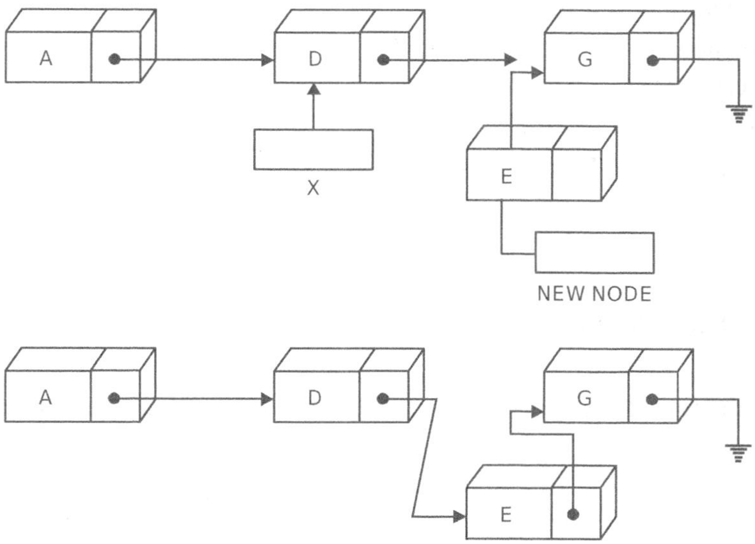

(Linked List with New Node)

Fig. 12.16

General Function for Insertion in between

```
node *add (node *FIRST, data-type OBJECT)
{
   node *X;
   node *X1;
   X = newnode;
```

```
    X -> DATA = OBJECT;
    X1 = FIRST;
    while (X1!=NULL)
{
    if(X -> DATA == OBJECT)
{
    X -> LINK = X1 -> LINK;
    X1 -> LINK = X;
    break;
}
    X1 = X1 -> LINK;
}
    return(FIRST);
}
```

Insertion at the End

Algorithm for Insertion at the End

Steps :

1. If AVAIL = NULL
   print "Overflow" go to step 10
2. X = newnode
3. Read (OBJECT)
4. X1 = First
5. While (X1< >NULL) repeat step 6
6. X1 = X1 –> LINK
7. X –> DATA = OBJECT
8. X1 –> LINK = X
9. X –> LINK = NULL
10. END

Let us explain the algorithm of insertion of element at end with the help of following pictures :

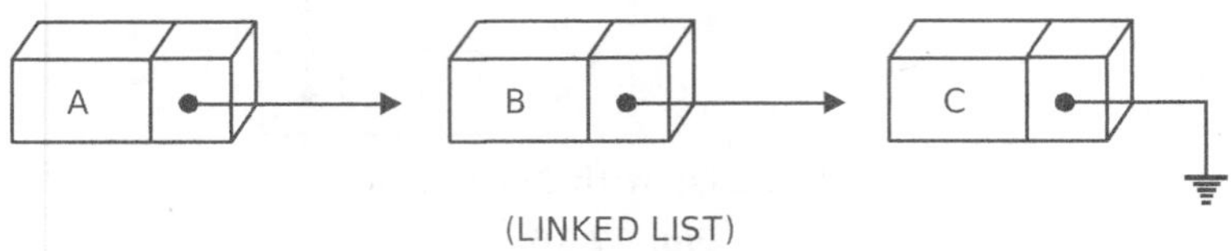

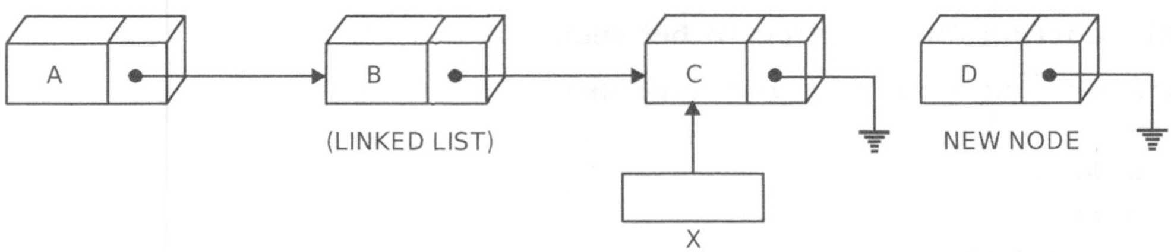

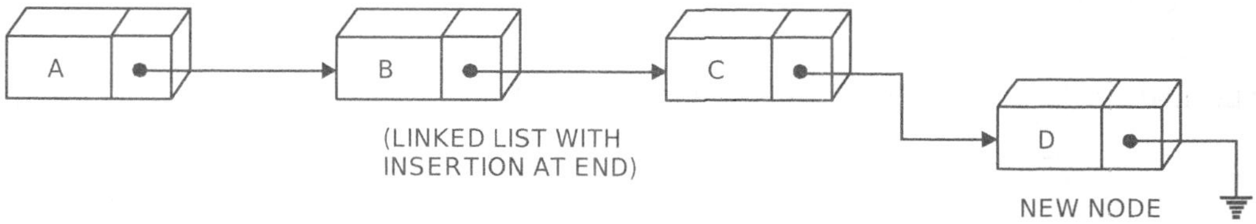

Fig. 12.17

General Function

```
node * add(node * FIRST, data_type OBJECT)
{
    node * X;
    node * X1;
    node * LAST;
    X = newnode;
    X -> DATA = OBJECT;
    X -> LINK = NULL;
    LAST = FIRST;
    X1 = FIRST -> LINK;
    while(X1!=NULL)
{
    LAST = X1;
    X1 = X1 -> LINK;
}
    LAST -> LINK = X;
    return(FIRST);
}
```

Deletion

Deletion of the element takes place on the same lines as insertion.

(*i*) Deletion in the beginning

(*ii*) Deletion in between (at desired location)

(*iii*) Deletion at the end of list.

Deletion in the Beginning

Algorithm of Deletion

Steps :

1. if (FIRST = NULL)
   print "LIST EMPTY" go to step 6
2. X = FIRST
3. FIRST = FIRST -> LINK
4. X -> LINK = NULL

5. Delete X
6. END

The node X is to be deleted in the above algorithm.

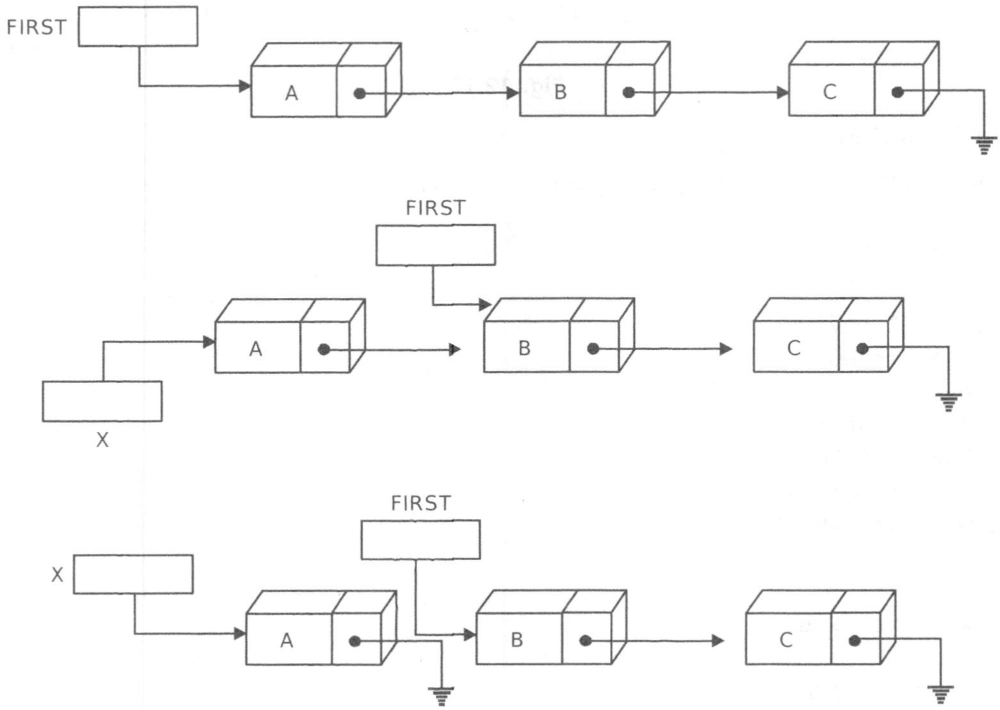

(Deletion in the Beginning)

Fig. 12.18

The deleted node from the memory can be deleted using delete() function.

Function for deletion at Beginning in a linked list

```
node * del(node *FIRST, data_type & OBJECT)
{
    node *X;
    X = FIRST;
    if(FIRST==NULL)
{
    printf("LIST EMPTY")&OBJECT = -1;
}
    else
{
    OBJECT = X -> DATA;
    FIRST = FIRST -> LINK
    X -> LINK = NULL;
```

```
        delete (X);
    }
        return (FIRST);
    }
```

Deletion of Element in Between

Algorithm for Deletion in Between

Steps :

1. if (FIRST = NULL)
   print "LIST EMPTY" go to step 7
2. FAR = First
3. X = FIRST -> LINK
4. while (X < > NULL) repeat step 6
5. if (X -> DATA = OBJECT)
   FAR -> LINK = X -> LINK
   delete(X)
6. else
   Far = X
   X = X -> LINK
7. END

Suppose the element 'C' is to be deleted from the list.

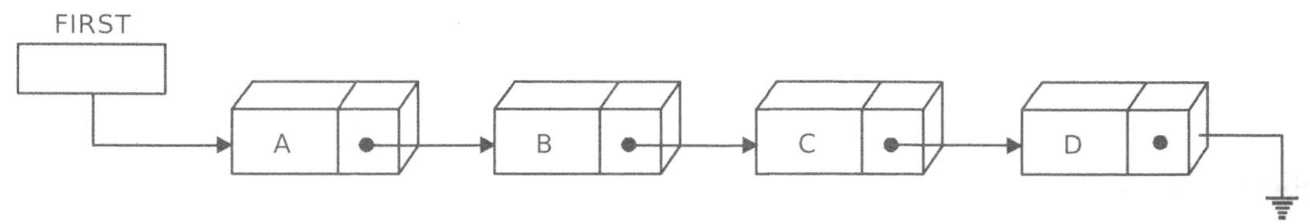

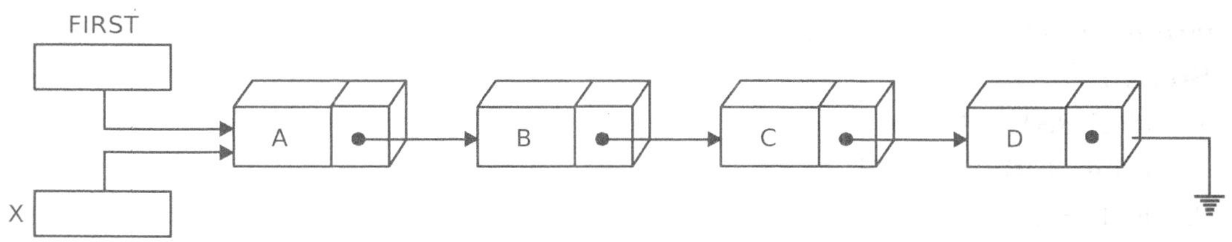

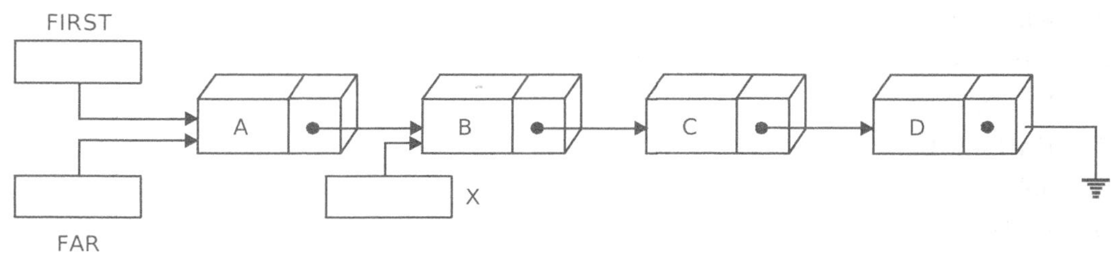

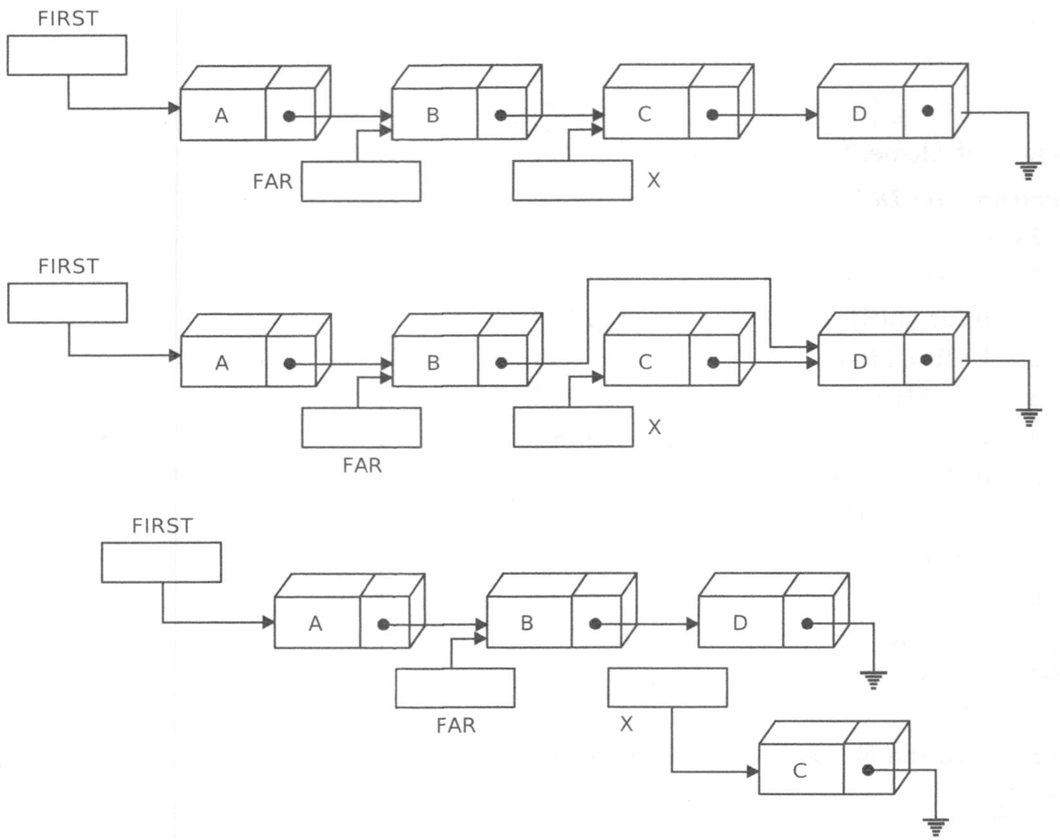

Fig. 12.19

Deletion at End

To delete a node from the end of a linked list, the node is traversed till the end of list.

Algorithm for Deletion at End

Steps :

1. if (FIRST = NULL)
   print "LIST EMPTY" go to step 9
2. FAR = FIRST
3. X = FIRST –> LINK
4. while (X < > NULL) repeat steps 5 to 8
5. Far = X
6. X = X –> LINK
7. FAR –> LINK = NULL
8. delete (X)
9. END

Let us explain the above algorithm with the help of pictures :

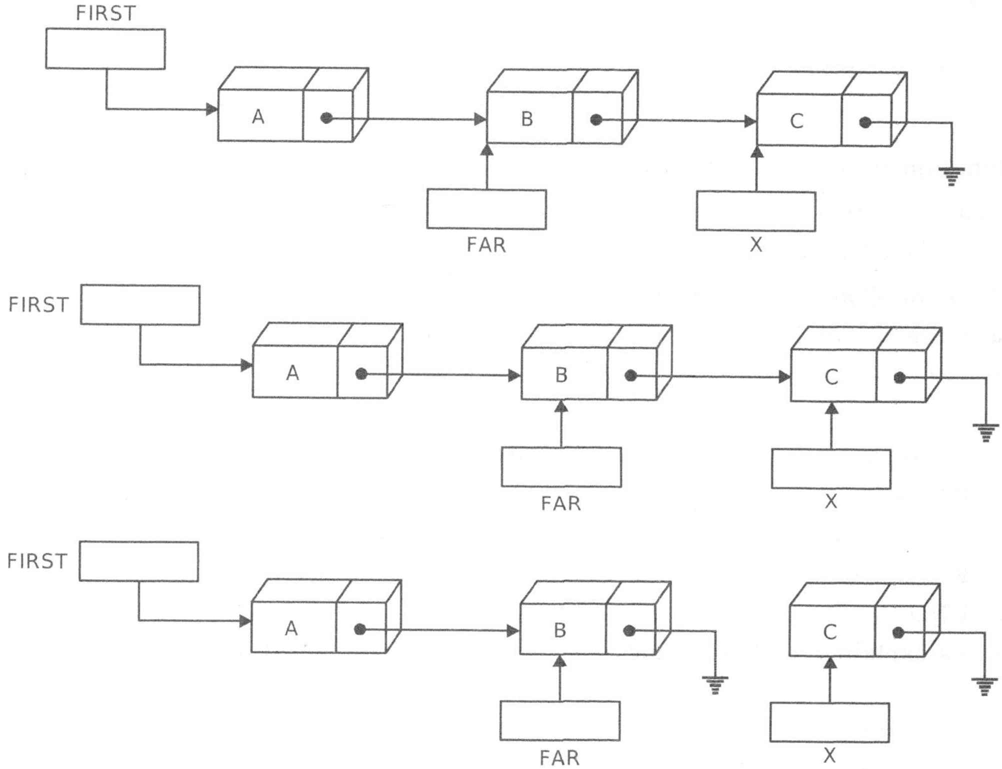

Fig. 12.20

General Function for Deletion at End

```
node *del(node *FIRST,data_type OBJECT)
{
   node *X;
   node *FAR;
   X = FIRST
   if(FIRST == NULL)
{
   printf("LIST EMPTY");
   OBJECT = -1;
}
   else
{
   while(X -> LINK! = NULL)
{
   FAR = X;
   X = X -> LINK;
}
   FAR -> LINK = NULL;
```

```
        OBJECT = X -> DATA
        delete(X);
    }
        return(FIRST);
    }
```

Concatenation of Two Linked Lists

Concatenation of two linked lists means combining two linked lists.

Two linked lists can be combined with each other.

Algorithm for Concatenation of Two Linked Lists

Suppose L and L1 and are two linked lists to be concatenated.

Steps :

1. X = L
2. while (X < > NULL) repat steps 3 and 4
3. FAR = X
4. X = X -> LINK
5. FAR -> LINK = L1
6. END

Let us explain the above algorithm with the help of pictures.

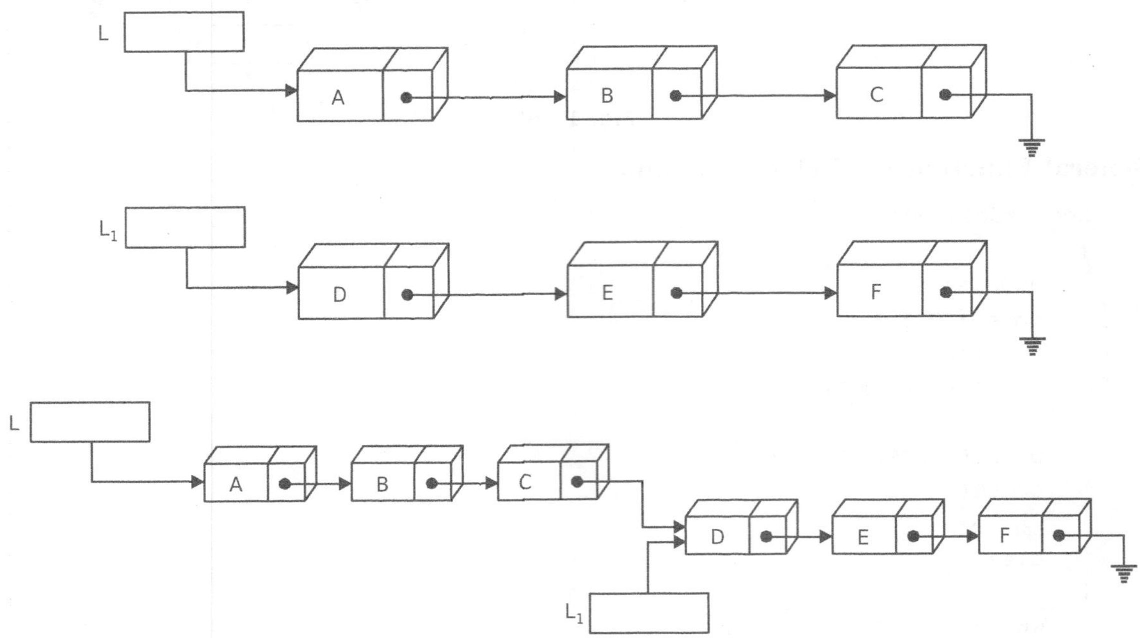

Fig. 12.21

Splitting of a Linked List

A linked list can be broken in to two independent linked lists.

Algorithm for Splitting a Linked List

Steps :

1. if (FIRST = NULL)
   print "LIST EMPTY" go to step 9
2. X = FIRST
3. FAR = FIRST
4. while (X < > NULL) and (X -> DATA < > OBJECT) repeat steps 5 and 6.
5. FAR = X
6. X = X -> LINK
7. if (X = NULL)
   print "NO SUCH NODE EXISTS"
8. else
   FIRST = X
   FAR -> LINK = NULL
9. END

Let us explain the splitting of a linked list with the help of pictures :

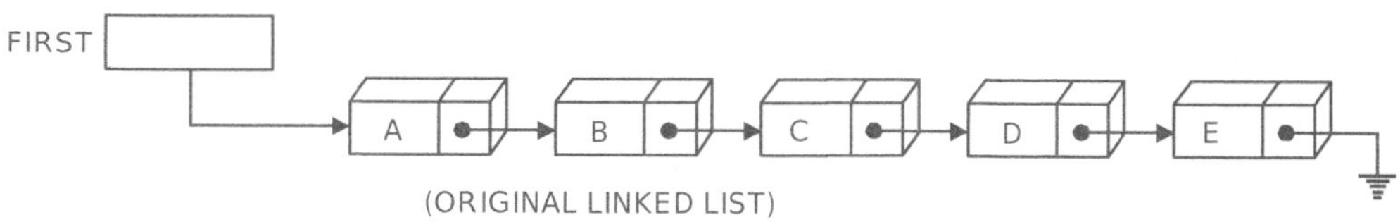

(ORIGINAL LINKED LIST)

Fig. 12.22. Original Linked List

Suppose this linked list is to be broken after the node having value C. Traverse the list until the node of value 7 is reached. This node is pointed as NULL. Store the address of next node in some other variable say NEW.

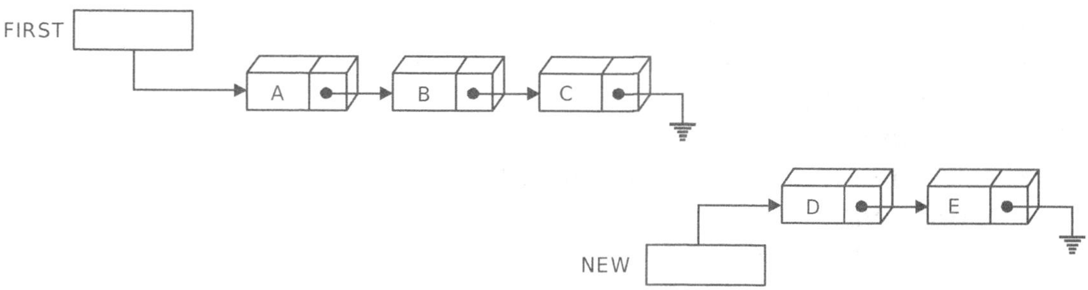

Fig. 12.23

Reversal of a Linked List

Reversal of a linked list means making the first node and the first node as the last node.

Algorithm for Reversal of a Linked List

Steps :

1. X = FIRST
2. if (FIRST = NULL) then
   print "LIST EMPTY" go to step 10.
3. New = X -> LINK
4. while (NEW < > NULL)
5. FAR = X
6. X = NEW
7. NEW = NEW -> LINK
8. X -> LINK = FAR
9. FIRST = X
10. END

Circular Linked List

Circular linked list means in which the last node of the list is pointing towards the first node instead of pointing to NULL.

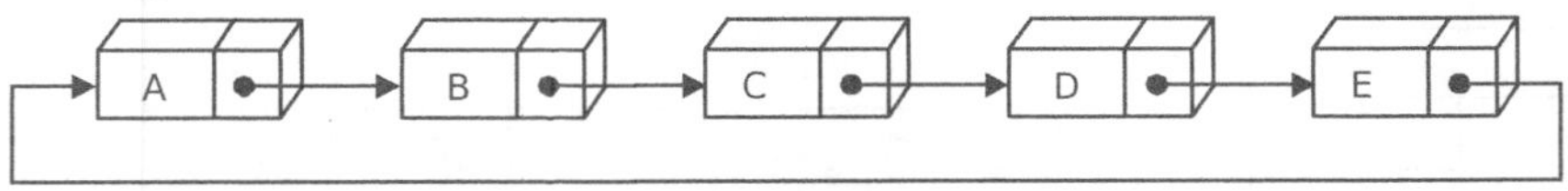

Fig. 12.24

Algorithm to Create a Circular Linked List

Steps :

1. if AVAIL = NULL then
   print "OVER FLOW" go to step 13
2. FIRST = NEW
3. AVAIL = AVAIL -> LINK
4. FIRST -> INFO = OBJECT
5. FIRST -> LINK = NULL
6. X = FIRST
7. for *i* = 1 to N–1 repeat steps 8 through 12
8. LAST = NEW
9. LAST -> INFO = OBJECT
10. LAST -> LINK = FIRST
11. X -> LINK = LAST
12. X = LAST
13. END

The above algorithm is based on the facts that a circular linked list contains N elements.

Each node of the list has two parts INFO and LINK. The first node is pointed by FIRST and last node points to the FIRST.

Chapter 1

Data Structures : Stacks

STACKS

We know that elements can be added to or deleted from any position in the array *i.e.,* in beginning, middle or end as the case may be. There may be some cases where the process of addition of deletion is required only at the end. A Stack, is a linear structure which is referred to as LIFO—Last in First Out. LIFO means that the goods/items received in the last are to be sold first.

Consider the case of a shopkeeper(grosser) where packets of washing soaps are received from the factory and kept in the shop one by one on the top of another in order of their arrival. Suppose there are 50 packets of soaps. The first packet is put on the floor. It attains 50th position when all the 50 packets are kept in order. The top most packet becomes the number one. The last packet becomes the number one packet and when sold, it becomes the first packet to be out.

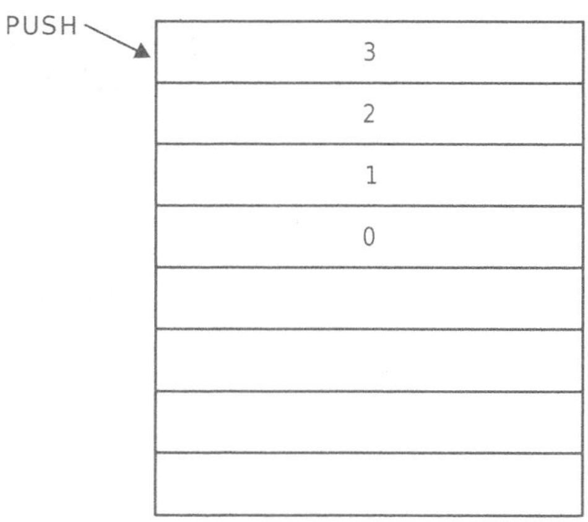

(*i*)

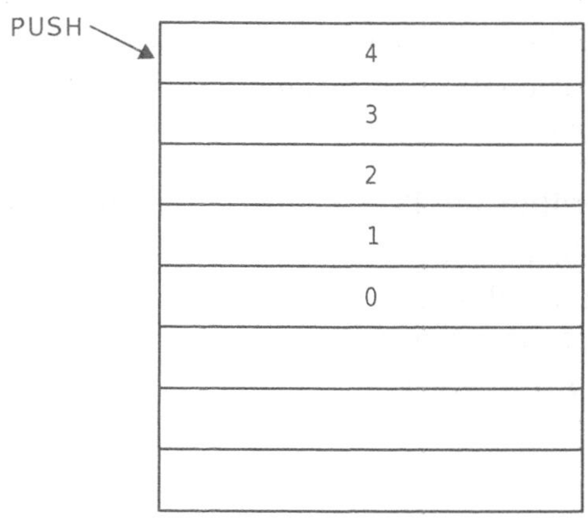

(*ii*)

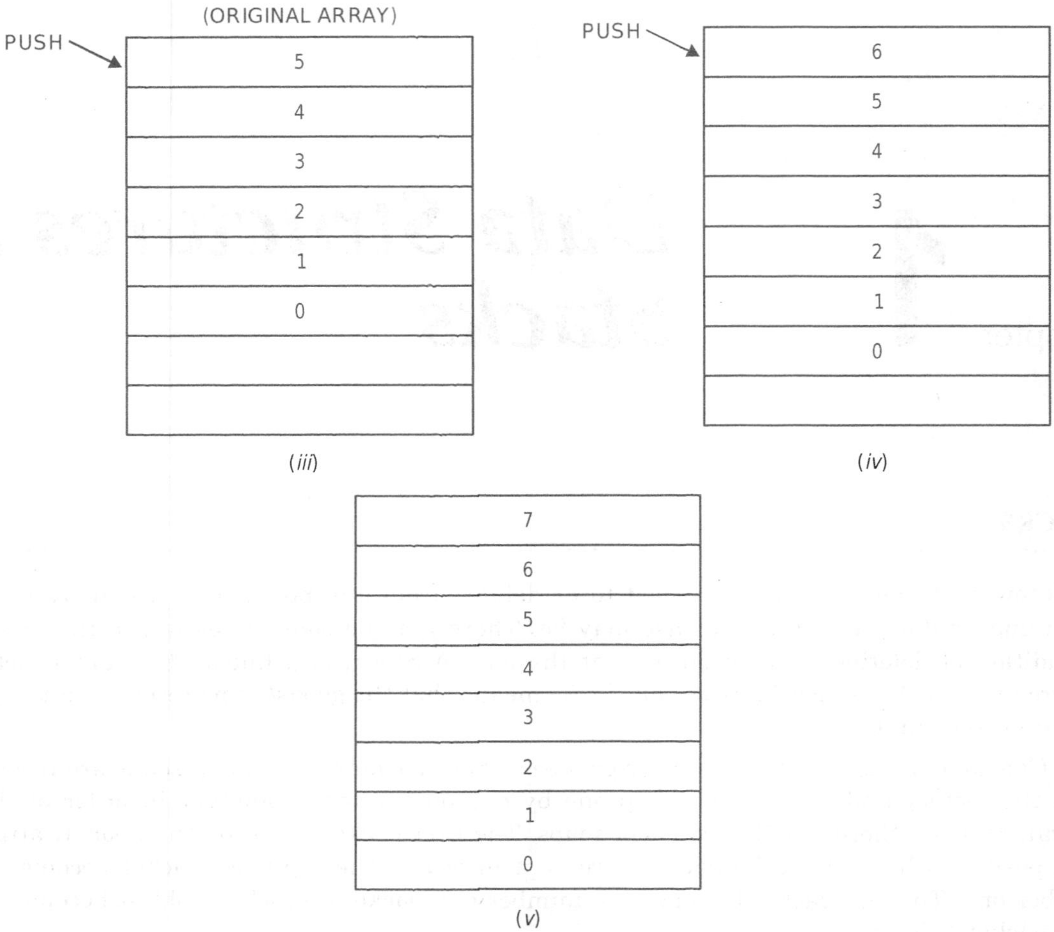

Fig. 13.1. Array Full Overflow

The diagram (*i*), (*ii*), (*iii*) and (*iv*) can accommodate the elements and are EMPTY Stack.

The situation in figure(*v*) is OVERFLOW as it can no more accommodate any further element.

Algorithm for PUSH Operation (Addition of Element)

Consider an array ARR[*n*] which can accommodate *n* elements is used for PUSH operation. An item OBJECT is to be inserted in this array. If TOP is less than *n* elements, it will allow PUSH operation otherwise not.

Step No. 1

if TOP > = *n*

go to Step No. 4

Step No. 2

TOP = TOP + 1

Step No. 3

ARR[TOP] = OBJECT

Step No. 4

END

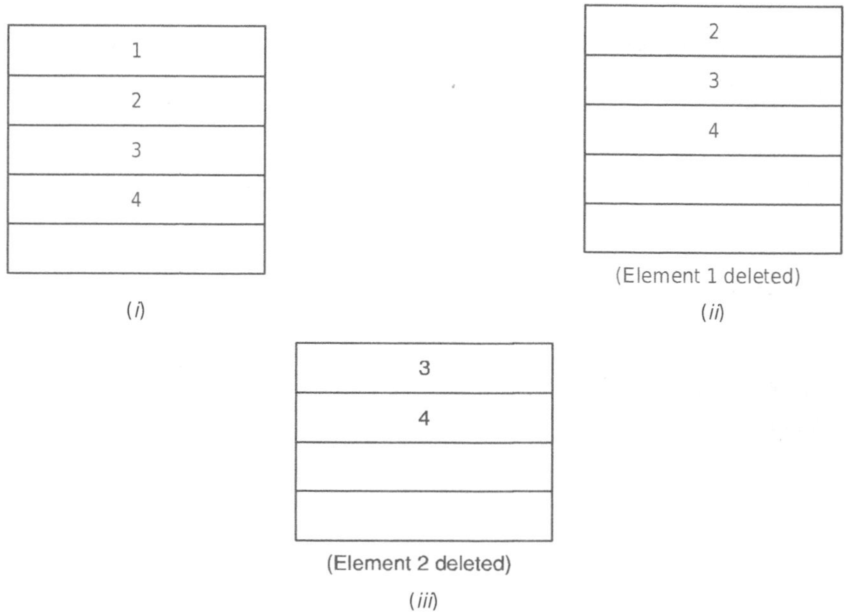

Fig. 13.2

Program : *Stack Implementation.*

```
#include<stdio.h>
#include<stdlib.h>
#define SIZE 10
void push(int i);
int pop(void);

int *top, *p1, stack[SIZE];
int main(void)
{
    int value;
    top = stack; /* top points to the top of stack */
    p1 = stack;
    do {
       printf("Enter element:: ");
       scanf("%d",&value);
       if(value!=0) push(value);
       else printf("Value on top is=%d\n",pop());
    } while(value!=-1);
    return 0;
}
```

```
void push(int i)
{
    p1++;
    if(p1 == (top+SIZE)) {
        printf("Stack Overflow!\n");
        exit(1);
    }
    *p1 = i;
}

int pop(void)
{
    if(p1 == top) {
        printf("Stack Underflow!\n");
        exit(1);
    }
    p1--;
    return *(p1+1);
}
```

```
/* Program on Stacks using array*/
#include<stdio.h>
#include<conio.h>
#include<stdlib.h>
#define MAX 10
int top = -1;
int stack_arr[MAX];
int push();
int pop();
int display();
int main()
{
    int choice;
    while(1)
    {
        printf("1.Push\n");
        printf("2.Pop\n");
        printf("3.Display\n");
        printf("4.Quit\n");
        printf("Enter your choice : ");
        scanf("%d",&choice);
        switch(choice)
        {
            case 1:
            push();
```

```
            break;
            case 2:
            pop();
            break;
            case 3:
            display();
            break;
            case 4:
            exit(1);
            default:
            printf("Wrong choice\n");
        }
    }
}

int push()
{
    int pushed_item;
    if(top == (MAX-1))
    printf("Stack Overflow\n");
    else
    {
        printf("Enter the item to be pushed in stack : ");
        scanf("%d",&pushed_item);
        top=top+1;
        stack_arr[top]=pushed_item;
    }
} /*End of push()*/

int pop()
{
    if(top == -1)
    printf("Stack Underflow\n");
    else
    {
        printf("Popped element is : %d\n",stack_arr[top]);
        top=top-1;
    }
}

int display()
{
    int i;
    if(top == -1)
    printf("Stack is empty\n");
```

```
    else
    {
        printf("Stack elements :\n");
        for(i=top; i>=0; i--)
        printf("%d\n",stack_arr[i]);
    }
}
```

2. Deletion of Element (POPPING)

Element can be deleted from a stack from the top only. The deletion operation is called POPPING. When all the elements are popped, the stack becomes totally EMPTY.

Algorithm for POPPING OPERATION

Consider an array ARR[n] which has n elements. (If it has no element, it is empty). Suppose an item OBJECT is to be deleted from this array.

Step No. 1

if TOP < = n

go to Step No. 4

Step No. 2

TOP = TOP – 1

Step No. 3

ARR[TOP] = OBJECT

Step No. 4

END

Arithmetic Operations in Stacks

The arithmetic operators which can be used in stack operations are mentioned below :

Symbol	*Meaning*	*Example*
*	Multiplication	a*b
/	Division	a/b
+	Addition	a+b
–	Subtraction	a–b
^	Exponentation	a^b

The following points must be noted regarding arithmetic operations.

1. Two arithmetic operators cannot be combined in continuation.
2. Operators contained in parenthesis are evaluated first and if parenthesis are nested, the innermost is evaluated first.
3. Two expressions connected by an arithmetical operator is also an expression. *Infix, Prefix, Postfix Notations.*

The expression in which the operator is placed between operands is called INEFIX expression.

The expression in which the operator is placed before its operands is called PREFIX expression and where the operator is placed after its operands is called POSTFIX expression.

Examples :

Infix Notations

1. $a + b$
2. $a - b$
3. $a + b - c$
4. $(a - c)/b$
5. $(a + b)/(b - d)$

   etc.

Prefix Notations

1. $+ab$
2. $+a*bc$
3. $+/a + bc*d - ef$
4. $*-ab$

   etc.

Postfix Notations

1. $ab +$
2. $abc*+$
3. $ab + c*$
4. $ab + cd +/$

   etc.

Conversion of Infix Expression of Postfix Expression

The following steps are used to convert an infix expression to a postfix expression :

1. Insert the braces to an infix expression after determining the desired order of evaluation.
2. The expression in the innermost braces should be converted into postfix expression by putting the operator after the operands.
3. The second step is repeated till the entire expression is converted into postfix expression while writing the resulting postfix expression, remove the braces.

Order of Priority

1. Brackets/Parentheses
2. Expoventation

   → (Topmost)

3. Division
4. Multiplication

   → (Middle)

5. Addition
6. Subtraction } → (Lower)

Algorithm to Convert Infix Expression to a Postfix Expression

Suppose an expression A is an arithmetic expression which has been written in infix notation. The following algorithm converts A of infix notation to A of postfix notation.

Step 1 : Push ("onto stack, and add")" to the end of A.

Step 2 : Scan A from left to right. Repeat steps through 3 to 6 for each elements of A till the stack is empty.

Step 3 : If an operand is encountered, add it to A.

Step 4 : If a left parentheses is encountered, then push it onto the stack.

Step 5 : If an arithmetic operator is encountered, then

(*i*) Repeatedly pop from the stack and add to A each operator (onto the top of stack) which has the same precedence than the operator.

(*ii*) Add the operator to the stack

Step 6 : If a right parentheses is encountered, then

(*i*) Repeatedly pop from the stack and add to A each operator (onto the top of the stack) until the left parentheses is encountered.

(*ii*) Remove the left parentheses but it is not to be added to A.

Step 7 : End

Illustration 1. *How would you evaluate a postfix expression 65+9* (without using braces)*

Solution :

The following figure represents the evaluation of the postfix expression :

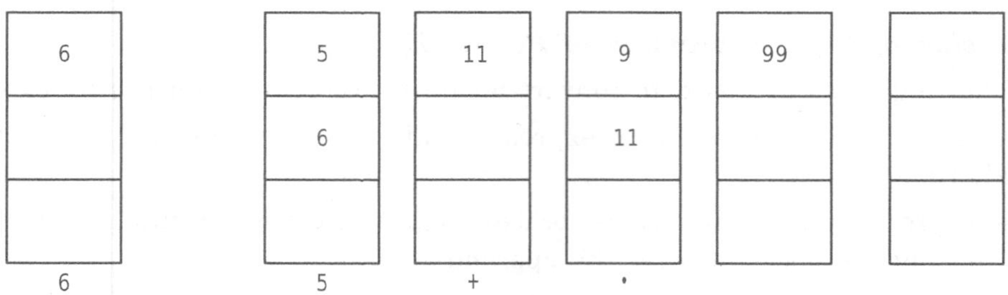

Fig. 13.3

In this expression first element *i.e.,* 6 is read and pushed onto the stack. Second element 5 is also pushed onto the stack in a similar way. The operator + pops these two elements off the stack. This operator produces their sum and this sum *i.e.,* 11 is pushed onto the stack. The next element 9 is read and pushed onto the stack. Thereafter the last operator + pops the top two elements and generates the product of 11 and 9 and the result 9 is pushed back onto the stack.

Illustration 2. *Give the postfix form of expression NOT A OR NOT B NOT C.*

Solution :

The evaluation order is ((NOT A) OR((NOT B) AND(NOTC)))

Priority order is

NOT
AND
OR

= ((A NOT) OR((B NOT) AND (C NOT)))

= ((A NOT) OR ((B NOT C NOT AND))

= A NOT B NOT C NOT AND OR

Illustration 3. *Convert the following infix expression to postfix form :*

*A + B*C + D in tabular form.*

Solution :

Input Element	*Stack*	*Output(Postfix)*
A		A
+	+	A
B	+	AB
*	*+	AB
C	*+	ABC
+	+	ABC*+
D	+	ABC*+D+
		ABC*+D+

MORE WORKED-OUT EXAMPLES

Example 1. *Given a stack as an array of 6 elements :*

(i) When will overflow take place ?

(ii) Can 'Z' be popped before 'T'. Give a reason for your answer.

Solution :

(*i*) Overflow in a stack takes place when TOP>N. Here N is the number of elements. When more elements than the limit of array are entered into the array, the situation of overflow takes place.

(*ii*) No, in no case Z can be popped before T. In a stack, all insertions or deletions take place from one end only *i.e.,* Top. Here the element Z is at the bottom, therefore, it cannot be popped before T.

Example 2. *Convert the following infix expression into postfix form-(P-Q) / R*(S-T)+U*

Solution :

Given expression is

(P-Q)/R*(S-T)+U

Converting the above expression

PQ-/(R*ST– +U)

PQ-/(RST–*+U)

PQ-/RST–*U+

PQ-RST–*U+/

is the postfix form.

❑❑❑

Chapter 1

Data Structures : Queue

QUEUE

A queue is a FIFO (First in First Out) structure represented as an array or linked list unless otherwise stated or implied, with the restriction that addition or deletion of the elements can be done at the ends only and not in the middle.

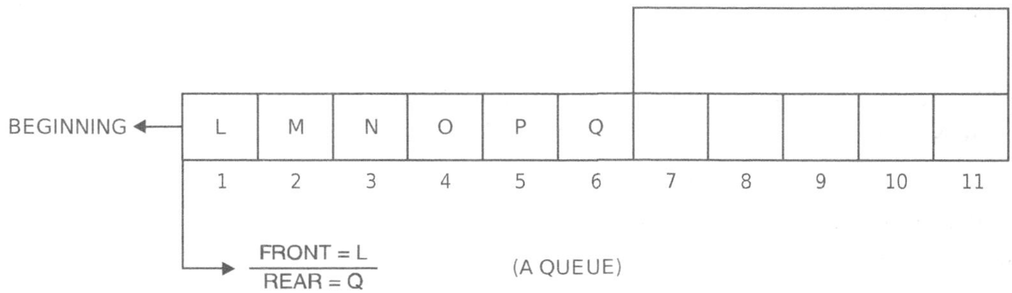

Fig. 14.1

The beginning of the array is called **Front**-end and the ending part of the array is called **Rear**-end. The terms front and rear are used while representing a single ended array *i.e.,* linear array. The element entered first is stored at the front and the last element is stored at Rear. If the value of front and the rear is known, we can know the number of elements in the queue can be ascertained.

Position of the Elements

(*a*) Position of the element is added to the queue, the value of rear is increased by 1.

Rear = Rear + 1;

(*b*) When an element is deleted from the front, the value of **Front** is increased by 1.

Front = Front + 1;

(*c*) If Front = Null *i.e.,* 0 then the number of element in the queue is **Zero** *i.e.,* the queue is totally empty.

Points to Note : We can also say

(*i*) When, Front = 0, Rear = –1, Queue is empty.

(*ii*) When, Front = Rear, Rear, there is exactly one element in the queue.

(when queue is implemented like an array)

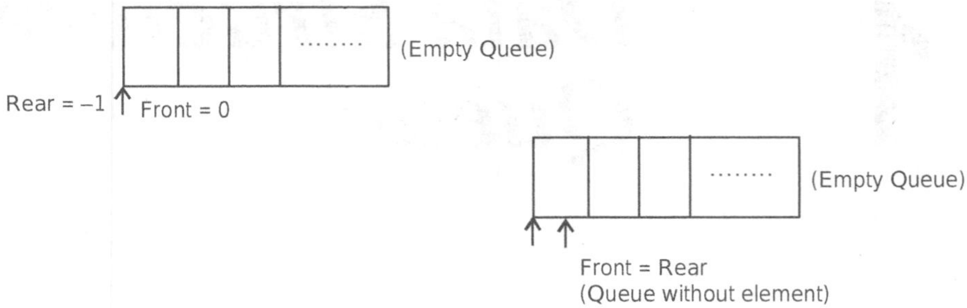

Fig. 14.2

Algorithm for Inserting an Element in a Linear Queue

Consider a queue having space for *n* elements. When n elements are filled in that queue, the queue becomes **Full**. Suppox an item OBJECT is to be inserted.

Step No. 1

if rear = n

write "Queue is full. Overflow Position" and return to end

Step No. 2

else

(find the new value of the rear)

Step No. 3

if front = null (queue is empty)

front = 1

rear = 1

Step No. 4

else

rear = rear + 1

Step No. 5

Queue[rear] = OBJECT

Step No. 6

Return

Step No. 7

END

Algorithm for deletion of an Element from the Queue

Step No. 1

if front = null

Write "queue is empty" and return

Step No. 2

else OBJECT = Queue[front]

Step No. 3

if front = rear

front = null

rear = null

Step No. 4

else

front = front + 1

Step No. 5

Return

Step No. 6

END

Program

```
//Operations on a Queue
   #include <stdio.h>
   int select();
   void create();
   void insertelement();
   void deleteelement();
   void display element();
   int m,n = 15, front t = 0, queue[15],rear = 0, object;
   int present;
   main()
   {
      int choice;
      do
      {
         choice = select();
         switch(choice)
         {
            case 1: createelement();
            continue;
            case 2: insertelement();
            continue;
```

```
            case 3: deleteelement();
            continue;
            case 4: displayelement();
            continue;
            case 5: puts("END");
            exit(0);
         }
      } while(choice!=5);
   }
   int select()
   {
      int selection;
      do
      {
         puts("Press 1: Create the queue"):
         puts("Press 2: Insert elements in the queue");
         puts("Press 3: Delete an element from the queue");
         puts("Press 4: Display the list");
         puts("Press 5: End");
         puts("Press your choice");
         scanf("%d",&selection);
      } while(selection<1 || selection>5);
      return selection;
   }
   void create( )
   {
      puts("Insert Elements in the queue");
      scanf("%d",&present);
      puts("Enter elements");
      if(front==0):
   {
      front++;
      scanf("%d",&object);
      queue[front] = object;
      rear = front;
   }
   do
   {
      ++rear;
      if(rear>present)break;
      scanf("%d",&object);
      queue[rear] = object;
   } while(rear<present);
   }
```

```
void insert element()
{
   rear++;
   if(rear>n){puts("Queue is full);exit(0);}
   puts("Enter number to be inserted");
   scanf("%d",&object);
   queue[rear] = object;
}
void deleteelement()
{
   if(front==rear){puts("The queue is empty");
   exit(0);}
   front ++;
   item = queue[front];
   if(front==n){front=1;rear=1};
}
void displayelement()
{
   for(m=front;m<=rear;++m)
   printf("%d\n",queue[m];
}
```

Circular Queue—Linked Implementation

A circular queue is that in which elements are arranged in a circular manner.

When the rear end of the queue joins the front end of the queue, it becomes a circular queue.

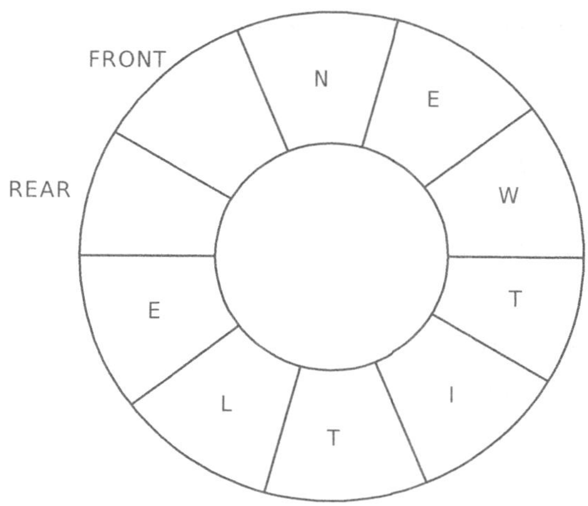

Fig. 14.3

Algorithm for Insertion in Circular Queue

Suppose Item OBJECT is to be inserted in a circular queue.

Step No. 1

if front = rear + 1
Write "Queue is full" and return

Step No. 2

else
if front = null
Write "Queue is empty"
front = 1
rear = 1

Step No. 3

else if rear = n
rear = 1

Step No. 4

else
rear = rear + 1

Step No. 5

Queue[rear]=OBJECT

Step No. 6

Return

Step No. 7

END

Algorithm for Deletion from a Circular Queue

Step No. 1

if front = null
Write "Queue is empty" and return

Step No. 2

else OBJECT = Queue[front]

Step No. 3

if front = rear
front = null
rear = null

Step No. 4

else if front = n
front = 1

Step No. 5

else front = front + 1

Step No. 6

Return

Step No. 7

END

Program

```
//Insertion and deletion in a circular list
#include <stdio.h>
int select();
void insertelement();
void deleteelement();
void displayelement();
int m,n=2,front,queue[15],q[15],rear,object,last;
main()
{
   int choice;
   do
{
   choice = select();
   switch(choice)
{
   case 1: insertelement();
   continue;
   case 2: delete element();
   continue;
   case 3: display element();
   continue;
   case 4: puts("END");
   exit(0);
}
}  while(choice!=4);
}
   int select()
{
   int selection;
   do
{
   puts ("Press 1 : Insert Element in the Circular queue");
   puts ("Press 2 : Delete element from the Circular queue");
   puts ("Press 3 : Display the list");
   puts ("Press 4 : End");
   puts ("Press your choice");
```

```
    scanf  ("%",&selection);
    }
}
    void insertelement()
{
    if((front==1 && rear == n) || (front == rear + 1))
    puts("Queue is Full",);
    else
{
    if(front==0){
    rear=1;front=1;}else
    if(rear==n)
    rear = 1; else rear++;
    puts("Enter Element to be inserted");
    scanf("%d", &item);
    queue[rear]=item;
    last++;
    queue[last]=item;
}
}
    void deleteelement()
{
    if(front==0)puts("Queue is empty!");
    else
{
    if(front==rear)
    {front=0;rear=0;last=0;}else
    if(front==n)
    {front=1;last=n-1;}else front++;
    item = queue[front];
}
}
    void displayelement()
{
    for(m = front; m<=last;++m)
    printf("%d\n",queue[m]);
}
```

DEQUE

In case of a queue, element can be added or deleted at one end. A deque is an abstract data type having data items to which items may be added or deleted at both ends (but not in the middle). The following operations can be done on the deque.

(*i*) add at front
(*ii*) add at rear
(*iii*) delete at front
(*iv*) delete at rear.

Declaration of Deque

```
struct deque
{
    data_type data;
    deque * forward, *backward;
}
deque * front, * rear;
```

Linked List Implementation of Queue

Linked Queue are the queues which have linked among their elements. In linked implementation two pointers front and rear are maintained for front and rear end of the queue.

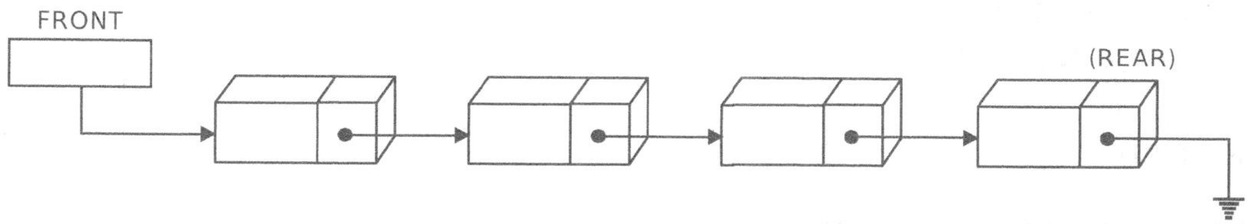

Fig. 14.4. A linked queue

Declaration of Linked Queue

```
struct node
{
    datatype data;
    node *LINK;
}
    node *front, *rear;
```

Insertation in a Linked Queue

Insertion in a linked queue takes place at the 'rear' end.

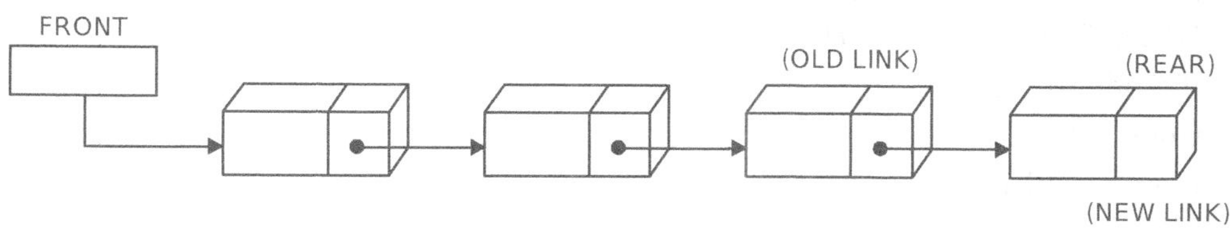

Fig. 14.5. Insertion is a linked queue

Algorithm of Insertion in Linked Queue

Steps :

1. If (AVAIL = NULL)
   Print "Overflow" go to step 8
2. NEWPTR = new node
3. Read(OBJECT) // item OBJECT to be inserted
4. NEWPTR –> DATA = ITEM
5. NEWPTR –> LINK = NULL
6. if (rear = NULL)
   {
   rear = NEWPTR
   front = rear
   }
7. else
   {
   rear –> LINK = NEWPTR
   rear = NEWPTR
   }
8. END

Deletion of Element in a Linked Queue

Deletion of element in a linked queue takes place at the front part.

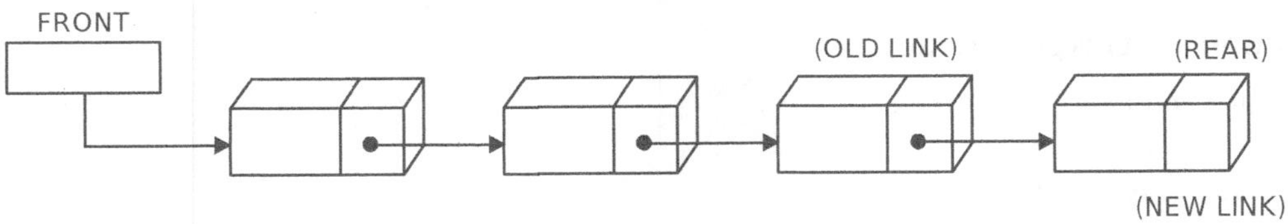

Fig. 14.6. Insertion is a linked queue

Algorithm for Deletion in a Linked Queue

Steps :

1. if front = NULL
   print "Queue Empty" goto step 5
2. OBJECT = front –> DATA
3. if front = rear
   front = NULL
   rear = NULL
4. else
   front = front –> Link
5. END

❑❑❑

Index

❑❑❑